Beyond Westminster

Paddy Ashdown was born in New Delhi, India, in 1941. At the age of four his family returned from India to farm in Ulster. After attending Bedford School, he became an officer in the Royal Marines and later commanded a unit of the Special Boat Section in the Far East, serving from 1959 to 1972, on active service in the Gulf, the Far East and Northern Ireland, and learning Mandarin Chinese while in Hong Kong. Joining the Foreign Office in 1972, he was posted to the British Mission to the United Nations in Geneva. In 1976 he returned to Britain to stand as Liberal candidate in Yeovil. He worked in local industry in the Yeovil area until 1981 and then, after a period of unemployment, as a youth worker for the Dorset county council youth service, responsible for initiatives to help the young unemployed.

He fought the Yeovil seat for the Liberals in 1979 and again, successfully, in 1983, serving as MP for Yeovil in the House of Commons since that date. In July 1988, following the merger of the Liberals and the Social Democrats, Paddy Ashdown was elected leader of the new Liberal Democrat Party on a ballot of all party members.

He married Jane in 1962; they have a daughter, Kate, and son, Simon.

BEYOND WESTMINSTER

Finding Hope in Britain

◆

PADDY ASHDOWN

S I M O N   &   S C H U S T E R

LONDON·SYDNEY·NEW YORK·TOKYO·SINGAPORE·TORONTO

First published in Great Britain by Simon & Schuster Ltd, 1994
A Paramount Communications Company

Copyright © Paddy Ashdown, 1994
First section of photographs copyright © Tony Pincham unless otherwise credited.
Second section of photographs copyright © Paul Reas unless otherwise credited.

Simon & Schuster Ltd
West Garden Place
Kendal Street
London W2 2AQ

Simon & Schuster of Australia Pty Ltd
Sydney

A CIP catalogue record for this book is available from the
British Library

ISBN 0–671–71340-X

Phototypeset in New Baskerville
by Intype, London
Printed and bound in Great Britain by
Butler & Tanner Ltd, Frome and London

To Shaheena

*If we can make it right for you,
we can make it right for
all of us.*

Contents

Acknowledgements

◆

These journeys would never have taken place had it not been for the help that I received from many friends and many who have become friends in the process.

The suggestion that I should make these journeys first came from Des Wilson, from whose generosity with his own ideas and prodigious abilities I have so often benefited. It was improved and made practical by Tim Clement-Jones and his team Gavin Grant, Simon Bryceson, Simon Titley, Dick Newby, Andrew Philips and Deepa Korea. That I have learned so much from these journeys owes a great deal to the hard work and careful thought they put in. I am especially indebted to Adrian Sanders, who organised my programmes with such skill and care.

Before I began these tours, I spent a series of 'study days' with experts in each of the subject areas I was to cover. Many who gave me the benefit of their views hold very different political views from my own. Most gave up substantial amounts of time and travelled long distances to do so. There are too many names to mention here, but I am grateful to them all for their generosity, for the information they gave me and for the suggestions about places I might visit.

What made each of these journeys special was the generosity of those who let me stay with them. They were, without exception, welcoming, fun to be with and unstinting with their help. I am indebted to them all, not just for their hospitality but also for their special insights: Ollie Goode and his family, Lis Burch, Rosemary and Doug Jones, Maureen McGuinness and her daughter, Jackie and Pat Aitcheson, John and Leslye Budge, Shamin Khan and her family, Mike Hoskin and the crew of the *Silver Harvester,* Jenny and Martin King, Eric and Lisa Bullick, John and Joan Alderdice, Winston and Pauline Simpson, the Lloyds of Cefn-y-Blaen, John and Carol Latham, David and Jane Walters, Judy and Ben in Peckham and Don and Celia Littlejohn.

The writing of this book has greatly benefited from the help and advice given by Steph Bailey, David Vigar, Alan Leaman, Carol O'Brien, Jennifer Kavanagh, Richard Holme, Les Farris and, especially, Nick South.

I am grateful, too, to my office staff, Clare Conway, Cathy Bakewell, Lisa Dorse, Simon Thompson, Deborah Chapman, Sarah Frapple and Sophie Conrad, who did so much of the arranging and re-arranging which was necessary to make this whole exercise possible and who often had to carry a considerable extra burden of work because of my absences; to Claire Margetts, who did such an exceptional job of typing out my notes and correcting the texts and, as always, to my wife Jane and my children who, in this as much as in so much else, gave me such patient and unfailing support.

None of these people bears any responsibility for the errors or failings in this book. Those are mine alone. But without their help I would have missed experiences which I shall treasure and from which I have learnt so much.

Introduction

◆

I intended these journeys as voyages of exploration. I think they have turned out to be a series of celebrations of the people I met on my travels.

I was elected to the House of Commons ten years ago, having had a number of jobs and, sometimes, no job at all. I had been a soldier, a diplomat, an industrial manager, a businessman, a youth worker and, on two occasions, one of the millions of unemployed. I did not plan it that way. But when I became an MP, I discovered that the things I had done were a good apprenticeship for my job in Parliament. They gave me a wide knowledge of the subjects on which I was going to be required to make decisions on behalf of my fellow citizens. Ten years later, that reservoir of knowledge, which I have found so useful, had become depleted. The first aim of these tours was to replenish it.

My second aim was to assess what I feared was becoming a growing gap between government and the governed in Britain. During the 1992 election campaign I travelled, I am told, the equivalent of once around the world, up, down and across Britain. But I saw almost nothing of the country, whose support I was asking for. My election tour usually consisted of flying into an airport from London, being whisked by car to a selected target audience, spending fifteen minutes with them and then being whisked on after conferring my 'Westminster blessing' upon them. I do not criticise those who organised this for me. This is the way it has to be in our modern politics and I believe that the organisers of my campaign gave me closer contact with the voters than the other two party leaders were able to enjoy.

But I was plagued by the thought that I did not really know about the true nature of the lives of those I was meeting and seeking the right to govern. So I promised myself that, after the election (when, I calculated, political life would be quieter!), I would do it again, only properly.

But, as it happened, after the election Britain plunged on into a frenetic round of politics, as though the election hadn't really happened. And I became more and more convinced that we in Westminster were speaking a language only we understood, doing things which were at best irrelevant to the lives of the people we were supposed to be serving, and too often that we were ignorant both of the conditions of people's lives and of the solutions they were coming up with to the problems they were experiencing.

This is not to criticise my fellow MPs. One of the great strengths of our otherwise rather flawed political system in Britain is that our legislators (or at least most of them) do have a very real, personal and regular contact with their constituents. But something strange seems to happen when we arrive in Westminster. As soon as we walk through those doors, whether in Government or in opposition, we seem to change from sensible people who know and care about the individuals we serve, to political robots. We suddenly start behaving in ways which most ordinary people find offensive and mouthing words that no sensible person believes in.

I have become more and more convinced that this dislocation between politics and real life is creating a dangerous and growing gap between politicians and people in Britain and other advanced Western democracies. I believe that what we have seen, with the rise of the extreme right in Europe, the phenomenon of Ross Perot in the United States and the growing disrespect for the Establishment everywhere, is an early sign of growing strains in our political and democratic system – maybe even the beginning of a crisis in our democracy itself.

And so I decided to leave the House of Commons for two and a half days every week in order to live and work with some of the different communities in our country. I hoped I would learn from this and I did – a lot. Many of my colleagues from other parties found this very perplexing and some found it risible. They believe, I presume, that politics can only be conducted in Westminster.

What I found in the places and people I visited was a Britain alive with new ideas and full of energy and determination. Even in the areas of deepest dereliction there are sparks of renewal which are ready to be fanned into flames. These journeys and visits have inspired me about what might be done if only we can find the means to unleash that raw energy.

Two and a half days a week is, of course, far too short a time. Another time I would want to make it longer. Nevertheless, it was better than the ten minutes I am normally allowed on a political leader's visit. What made each of these visits so valuable and informative to me, however, was the fact that I was alone and without the press (one wag commented that I was a 'leader with a detached retinue'!) and that the people who were kind enough to put up with me, allowed me also to live and work with them.

I did not want these journeys to be just one long whinge about the state of Britain. Indeed I deliberately did not go to just the 'problem' areas of our country. I had a hunch that, outside the close and fuggy atmosphere of Westminster, not only were there problems which we did not know of, but that there were also solutions to many of the problems that we in the House of Commons cannot find answers to. I leave it to you to decide whether that was correct.

Some of the words and descriptions in this book will offend – indeed some already have. I have come under considerable pressure to change what I have written so that it conforms more to 'political correctness' and the 'official view'. I have resisted this, believing that it is more important to reflect the views of the people I spoke to. In a few cases I have changed the names and obscured locations, but only where I have been asked to do so by those involved.

What I have tried to describe is things as they were when I visited, not as they necessarily are now. No doubt many things will have changed in the intervening months. I know, for instance, that considerable strides have now been taken to improve the situation in Hartcliffe and Withywood, that the regeneration of Moss Side is now underway and official police attitudes in Manchester are changing and that conditions in the North Peckham and Camden estates have improved since I visited.

I had originally intended to confine these journeys to Britain. However mid-way through my planned programme I went to Bosnia to visit British troops there and to return to Sarajevo.

What I saw there of the attitudes and actions of people from Britain so powerfully reinforced what I had seen elsewhere that I thought it right to include a chapter on this visit too.

I have divided this book into two parts. In the first, I have attempted to describe, in strict chronological order, what I saw and heard as I saw and heard it. Whenever possible I have tried to let people speak for themselves. I have also tried to keep my own views separate, though no doubt my viewpoint is plain enough. I do not vouch for the veracity of every fact, or the fairness of every description. I wanted to portray the conditions I witnessed not necessarily as they objectively are, but as they are seen by those who live in them. In the second part, I give my own conclusions and what I think should be done.

My aim has been to try to present to the interested and concerned citizen of Britain what some parts of our country are like at present and how one politician thinks we might change them for the better.

Chapter 1
'NFH'

16 November 1992

To Bristol to spend the day with Pat Mundy, the Development Manager of Hartcliffe and Withywood Ventures Ltd (HWV), an organisation funded jointly by the Government, city council and private firms, set up in 1985 to regenerate hope and jobs in the area. The Hartcliffe and Withywood estate houses 23,000 people.

◆

The deprivation in Hartcliffe and Withywood is not immediately visible.

Driving round the edge, as many Bristolians do every morning on their way to work, the estate looks rather better than many I have seen on the edge of Britain's cities. Typical fifties and sixties tower blocks, some scattered lower housing and wide-open spaces look green in the cold afternoon light of November. Last night's severe gales had blown away much of the rubbish which normally accumulates in these no man's lands. Against the gale's dying gusts, struggling figures push their way towards their destination, leaning into the wind with lowered heads.

Not an attractive sight. But normal for the conditions in which many in Britain live their lives. There was nothing here which seemed to justify or explain the explosive and destructive riots which, four months ago, blew up like a blast of wind and blew away just as quickly. But then the point about Hartcliffe and Withywood is that its deprivations are multi-layered and hidden. Neither the existence nor the depth of the problems are immediately visible to the casual eye.

But the local hospital doctors know of them. They write 'NFH' on personal medical records for this area. This means 'Normal For Hartcliffe'. It is the doctors' way of saying that, though the overall health indicators on the estate are more like those for a

Third World country, and would be a cause for concern elsewhere, they are not unusual for Hartcliffe and Withywood.

Barclays Bank knows it too. They shut the only remaining bank
on this estate a year ago because 'it wasn't making enough profit'.
And the Co-op knows it. Everyone believes they operate a different pricing system, charging people on Hartcliffe and Withywood
higher prices than they do in their more central stores. No doubt
this has nothing to do with the fact that most of the residents
here are trapped on the estate.

But they are. Car owners are a minority here and bus services
to anywhere but the centre are few and far between. Even the
act of mourning requires four buses. The cemetery is only two
miles away. But to get there by public transport means a bus to
the city centre and a second to the graveyard and the reverse
journey on the way back. Visiting a relative's grave for Hartcliffe
residents can be a whole day affair.

Lots of things have been promised to Hartcliffe and Withywood.
The Health Authority promised them a hospital thirty years ago,
the council promised them a leisure centre, someone promised
a supermarket and someone else a cinema. But none of them
has ever materialised.

Over the last two years they have applied for money from the
Government's City Challenge competition. A lot of effort went
into this and some exciting ideas came from the community
about how to reverse the decline. The process brought together
parts of the community who had never been together before;
hopes ran high. But they lost both years. They are now determined to continue on their own.

On the edge of the estate lies a huge complex of derelict
buildings. Now owned by Lord Hanson, they lie deserted, waiting
for property prices to rise again. This was the old Wills factory,
the source of jobs on this estate and many others in Bristol. Wills,
established in Bristol in the late eighteenth century, relied on
the skills and loyalty of Hartcliffe for many years and had a
reputation as a good employer. But in the late 1980s they suddenly closed down and left. Their legacy to their one-time work
force is this abandoned site which blights the area and a crop of
sixty-year-olds now suffering from smoking-related diseases as a
result of Wills' generosity in supplying free cigarettes to those in

work and a weekly cigarette allowance for past employees to supplement the Wills' retirement pension.

All these things have been explained to me by Pat Mundy and her two colleagues Brian McInally, the managing director of HWV, and Pat Waite, their training manager. Brian tells me that they have effectively 'lost a generation': those between twenty-five and thirty who were jobless in the last recession and are still jobless in this one. They have been so immersed in dependence and hopelessness that they are now, in his words, 'irrecoverable'.

Many of these make up Hartcliffe's second-shift people. For there are two different Hartcliffes, with two quite different sets of inhabitants. The original residents moved here thirty years ago from slum dwellings in the inner city. They were thrilled to have houses with bathrooms and gardens and beautiful views. And they had well-paid local jobs – until many of the local factories closed down. Those who came in later are mostly unemployed and many are single parents. The housing crisis has forced the city council to put families with children into tower blocks, often next door to 'problem families'; the drug addicts and the alcoholics who were already housed there.

These two communities live separate lives with different standards and opposite body clocks. They make up Daylight Hartcliffe and Withywood, and Darkness Hartcliffe and Withywood. The former sleep to avoid the day. The latter barricade their doors at night against the strange and violent land they live in after dark. Those who visit Hartcliffe and Withywood during the day see only one side of the estate. Those who live there, live with both.

Dawn, self-confident and articulate, has learnt to live with Daylight Hartcliffe and make the best of it. But she tells me that at night she has five locks each on the front and back doors and she bolts her internal doors, too. She says that there is no one she knows on the estate who has managed to avoid being a victim of crime in one way or another.

Dawn has a sixteen-year-old son and a young baby. Her son has already been in trouble with the police over drugs, which, Dawn tells me, are rife. The pushers sell to the children in the local school. Parents, teachers and police have tried to stop the trade, but don't seem to be able to. 'What hope is there for my son? There is no escape,' Dawn says. 'There is little or nothing here for youngsters and we are so isolated that the kids can never get away. They always have to mix with the same kids – so bad habits are bound to spread, aren't they?'

Pat Mundy explains that having a job means, among other things, having a second 'world' with a different peer group. But being permanently unemployed means being permanently trapped from childhood, through school, to the dole, in the same peer group – in Hartcliffe's case one in which drugs and crime prevail. She says that whatever she does to give youngsters a way out, they can never escape from the pressure pulling in the opposite direction from class and street mates.

Annis Fessey and her husband Brian are two Church of England curates, who moved into the area about a year before the riots. They have joined the rest of us in Pat Mundy's office in HWV's headquarters in the middle of the estate.

Annis tells me that the residents of Hartcliffe have largely abandoned politics; 'Why vote – they never do anything for us' is the common view. Turnout in local elections was below 30 per cent and at the last general election half of Hartcliffe didn't bother to vote.

But there is some new political activity on the estate. A National Front group has started up and Class War moved in during the riots, putting out glossy leaflets showing pictures of policemen being kicked, accompanied by approving slogans.

Annis and Brian have had experience of deprivation in other areas, but they were shocked by the hopelessness they had found in Hartcliffe. Annis says that over the last two or three years she has watched the community go steadily down hill. She warned of the probability of riots and disturbances more than a year ago. But no one paid any notice.

Annis introduces me to Sally, a young mother who has been lucky enough to find a job. When Sally was unemployed, she received benefit worth £176.90 a week for her family to live on. When she got a job she lost many of the benefits she had been entitled to. She now receives a wage of £45 per week from work, to which is added other benefit assistance worth £136, making a total of £181 in cash – £5.10 more than she would have received if she had stayed on the dole. But from this extra £5 a week she must pay travelling expenses. So her family is worse off now that she works than they were when she was on the dole. Sally is in the poverty trap which imprisons so many in hopelessness on this estate and hundreds of others like it across Britain. But she tells me 'I will continue with the job. I have less money to keep the family, but I do have my self respect.'

Downstairs a young man who has a degree in mechanical engineering is teaching other young unemployed people how to apply for jobs which they all know do not exist. He is a natural teacher and is doing his best to motivate his audience – but both teacher and pupils know that whatever his skill or their enthusiasm, the outcome is likely to be the same.

But there is a fight back beginning and it is coming not from outside, but from within the estate, helped and fostered by HWV. In a neighbouring room a group of volunteers are working on projects to improve the environment of the estate. Two of them have been unemployed for six years. They work for nothing because it gives them something to do and a sense of worth. They have recently cleared Strawberry Lane, an old forgotten pathway running through the estate which had been neglected by the local council and filled with cars and rubbish. They are proud of their work and the little victory they have won over despair and other people's neglect.

Meanwhile, a group of mothers are raising funds to build an adventure playground. And HWV will shortly be starting a child-care training programme and plan an after-school club to start in January 1993. They have also brought together a group of local builders to form a community business aimed at giving local people access to jobs on the construction work that the city council have promised on the estate.

And there are other signs of hope, too. Pat takes me to some small business units she has had put up in some neglected space near the centre of the estate. They are cheerful and bright amid the grey. There are seven of them and six are occupied by small businesses established by local residents. I meet Wilf and Mehdi who have started a small business making pine furniture. They are eager and full of hope. Next door is another small business restoring discarded furniture. Both businesses are just surviving despite the recession.

This project has been made possible because of funding from the Urban Programme. But while we are there, news comes through that the Government has announced that the Urban

Programme is to end. There are assurances from Whitehall that a new scheme will be put in its place. But here, in Hartcliffe and Withywood, there is suspicion and concern that, behind the Whitehall words, another promise is being betrayed.

Chapter 2
'Planning for Real'

17 November 1992

To visit the Community Lands Workspace Services (CLAWS) office in Collier Street, to spend a day with Michael Parkes, CLAW's community planner. During the day we visit the King's Cross railway lands development site and the two organisations putting forward plans to develop it: the local-resident-based Railway Land Development Group and the London Regeneration Corporation, a consortium of developers. In the afternoon, we visit the Boundary Estate in Spitalfields, a housing complex predominantly occupied by Bangladeshis. Later Michael takes me to see the Spitalfield Market development and then to the Brick Lane Community Development Trust.

◆

We are standing on a flat roof on the Maiden Lane estate in North London. We have come here to view the King's Cross development site. But Michael Parkes's first comments are about Maiden Lane itself.

'This estate was highly praised by architects and experts in the 1960s,' he tells me. 'But it's hell to live in now.' Around me are narrow alleyways which no doubt reminded the architects who designed it of their summer holidays in Cornish fishing villages and Tuscan towns. But here they have become havens for drug dealers and criminals. The area is impossible to police and terrifying to live in.

The flats are made up of a jungle of concrete balconies and walkways arranged on different 'interesting' levels. The flat roofs and walkways between them provide ideal access points for burglars. The concrete which must have looked so neat in the 1960s is now stained and cracking. The troughs designed for flowers have become depositaries for rubbish. The paint is peeling. The garages under the flats are full of derelict cars and dark spaces, menacing even in daylight. Narrow alleys, which doubtless were incorporated to provide intimacy and human scale, instead provide perfect cover for muggers and drug dealers. And everywhere there is spray-paint graffiti, the detritus of drug and solvent abuse and all the signs of a community which from the start had no chance of ownership or control over its own living space.

In Michael's nearby CLAWS office, he had showed me how things might have been done when they designed the estate. Michael and CLAWS have long promoted a planning process they call 'planning for real'. This involves architects abandoning their role as 'experts' who design things 'for' people and becoming instead consultants who enable people to design and shape their own environment for themselves. 'Who is better qualified to design an area, an architect brought in from outside, or the people who have to live there? The architects' job is not to give them the designer's dreams, but to enable them to realise their own,' Michael says.

He showed me a 1:200 scale architect's model that CLAWS has used in helping to redevelop Brick Lane, the deprived East End Bangladeshi area which we were going to see later in the day.

It was unlike any architect's model I had ever seen. Not the usual expensive, untouchable, perfectly constructed representation, much beloved of town planners and developers, but a child-like collection of moveable, rough constructions made of cardboard and silver paper, painted crudely to represent what things might be like. The purpose, Michael explains to me, is to encourage people to use and alter the model, and see it not as a mechanism for illustrating the architect's 'solution', but as a means for the community to express what it wants. The cruder and rougher the model, the more ordinary people without architect's skills (and sometimes without even the ability to read) feel able to play about with it to express their opinions.

Michael's colleague Lesley Klein showed me their 'stick a dot' system designed to enhance the process. Each visitor viewing the model during the phase of public consultation was given a sheet with coloured dots, corresponding to their views (red for disagree, green for agree etc.) They then stick these on boards accompanying the model which contain examples and propositions relating to the design and the positions of amenities such as gardens, benches or pedestrian crossings and so on.

In the past, consultation I have witnessed has been of the take it or leave it sort, designed not so much to hear people's views as to receive their objections. A process intended more for protest than for partnership. So I press Lesley and Michael for examples of successful 'planning for real'. Lesley told me of an approach they received from the Waterfield Tenants' Association in Hounslow.

Waterfield is a typical 1960s deck access estate. Three-storey blocks containing identical flats; open public space in between, owned by no one and therefore regarded as the responsibility of 'them' at the council; rubbish-blown public areas, threatening stairwells and bleak common walkways.

The tenants had lost all confidence in the council who, they said, never did anything for them, except impose their own schemes and rules, demand rent and ignore their complaints. The first thing CLAWS had to do was win back the tenants' confidence. They decided they couldn't do this unless they established a presence on the estate (council officials sitting in remote offices, telling the tenants what to do but never visiting the estate, had been one of the chief complaints). So CLAWS set up an old caravan on site as their office and dropped leaflets through the estate doors inviting people to visit them.

Slowly a bond was established with the residents, who began to see CLAWS were on their side, rather than the council's. Then the consultations began. The first task was to ask the residents their views. The problems came tumbling out.

The elderly complained that the low walls, which the architect had put in at the entrances to the buildings to help old people get down ramps and stairs, had become instead hiding places for children and muggers waiting to frighten them or worse. CLAWS had the walls taken down and replaced with metal bar fencing stout enough to provide support for the frail, but open enough to deny a hiding place to muggers. Others suggested fencing off the open public spaces in front of each block to create private gardens. But what sort of gardens? CLAWS suggested a visit to Kew.

Practically the whole estate turned out to go – families, children and the elderly all together. It was a real social occasion, as well as a learning one. Some of the youngsters talked for the first time to the elderly they had previously terrified. For many on the estate it was a chance to meet neighbours they didn't really know because they had all been cut off in their flats by the common enemy of the squalor and hostility outside.

It had been a great day. They began to see how and what to plant and returned to the CLAWS model to lay out their estate. Most of the re-planting in the estate had already been contracted out to professionals by the council, but the tenants were allowed to try their hand at what was left. The council's contractors told CLAWS that all this was a terrible waste of money; that the residents' planting would never survive the dry summer. Ninety per cent of the residents' plants survived. But the contractors had to return to replace 50 per cent of theirs.

Michael explained to me that there was nothing you could do to alter a fundamentally bad design. The basic structure of Waterside would stay the same. But the estate at least now had the feel that human beings lived, rather than took refuge there. Vandalism had almost disappeared as the residents and their children felt 'ownership' of their environment and the area had changed from being a ghetto for the unlucky and inadequate to becoming a sought-after place to live.

CLAWS used the same method to transform a Lambeth play-school yard from a tarmac waste land into a spectacular school garden for £28,000. Similar council refurbishments elsewhere had cost £100,000.

Later in the day I was to meet East End residents who had also been involved in this process. They told me that they had started off being frightened of the experts, until they had realised that they themselves were experts, too; not about building and con-struction, but about local conditions and what would and wouldn't work there. In the process of designing their own environment they had learnt new skills they never thought they had the ability to acquire and used power they never believed they would get the right to use.

Standing now on the roof of Maiden Lane, Michael says 'If the architects who designed this estate had asked the people who were to live here for their views, many of the current problems might never have arisen.'

From Maiden Lane, we drop down to the King's Cross railway lands development site itself. It was here that the industrial revolution came to London. Until the middle of the eighteenth century this area, then known as Battle Bridge, was largely open fields, dotted with inns and containing the original old St Pancras church. In 1756 a new road was built between Paddington and Islington. Residential development quickly followed and the London Smallpox and Fever hospital was built here, roughly where the present Great Northern Hotel stands today. The area quickly became infamous as a haunt of thieves and murderers. In 1845, the first redevelopment of King's Cross started with the demolition of the smallpox hospital and the building of a great railway terminus. Around this was constructed what must have been, in its time, a wonder of modern industrial design: two great railways stations, with their attendant hotels, railway workers' housing and marshalling yards and the tunnels and viaducts to connect them to each other and the north. Underneath, the Regent's Canal with two huge twin lock chambers and interchange facilities to transfer coal, grain, timber and food from trains and carriages for transport into the city and to take manure and refuse onto horse-drawn carts and barges travelling in the opposite direction. Here was a potato market, a German gymnasium, a two-level coal depot, a storage vault for Burton-upon-Trent beer, a revolutionary system of two-level hydraulic wagon hoists, a gas works, timber yards, a magnificent granary, the greatest span arched roofs of their time, covering passenger terminals and train sheds, and the most modern office blocks of their day.

Today, it is wasteland. What has not vanished of the old glory is crumbling fast. The community that lives around it is one of London's most deprived; poverty, prostitution and drugs prevail. But the site, all 135 acres of it, situated at the centre of London, is the possible location for a second Channel Tunnel terminus and represents one of the biggest and most valuable inner-city development sites in the world.

What should be done with it? Two groups are competing to provide an answer. Michael takes me first to meet the King's Cross Railway Lands Development Group. It is made up of local residents and community representatives who have worked with Michael and other architects to put together a scheme which provides low-cost housing, shopping areas, leisure and cultural facilities and a natural park. We meet in a semi-derelict community building which is unheated and we all stand round stamping our feet in the cold and cradling our mugs of tea in cupped hands while the crude model showing their ideas (made by a volunteer in his own bedroom), is explained to me. They want to enhance the run-down King's Cross area as well as provide the housing and facilities within reach of local residents which this area of London so badly lacks.

Afterwards we go onto the King's Cross site to visit the other development consortium, the commercial developers who make up the London Regeneration Corporation. Their offices are in one of the splendidly refurbished old canal-side Victorian buildings. They have spent five years and, it is said, £30 million preparing a plan designed to reap the highest economic value from the land. They have some interesting proposals and have recently followed the Railway Lands Group by including community projects and low-cost housing in their scheme. But I can't help thinking that the result will be a high-value office and residential area which will have to be protected from the King's Cross neighbourhood, rather than be a part of it.

Next Michael takes me to the Boundary Estate in Spitalfields. This is the original site of the infamous Jago, much written about by Charles Dickens, the worst slum in London in the nineteenth century and home to some of Jack the Ripper's atrocities.

Today it is home predominently to the Bangladeshi community. They live in the nineteenth-century blocks put up when the Jago was cleared. This was model housing in its day. Indeed, the estate has now been declared a conservation area, in recognition of its architectural significance. But that doesn't stop it looking like a prison and feeling like one too.

Oppressive outside, the houses are damp, miserable and overcrowded within. Most flats have broken windows and peeling walls. The Bangladeshi families who live there are desperately trying to maintain the family networks upon which their way of life is built. But against them laps a tide of criminality and drugs which erodes even the strongest of foundations: six or eight children to a flat, mothers and fathers working shifts and trying to snatch daylight sleep while their children play or attempt homework in the same room. There are many hundreds of children on the estate. But there is only a space of about sixty square yards for their play area. And everywhere the damp fugginess of too many human beings in too little space and the ever-present hacking coughs of young and old exposed to conditions which are perfect for the spread of respiratory disease.

We move on to Spitalfields Market, where I meet Eric Reynolds of Urban Space Management. He has been employed to make use of the old empty site of Spitalfields Market for the next few years, before the developers move in to knock it down and build sky-scraper office blocks. Avoiding blight is a key component in planning for a whole community. He has performed wonders in providing temporary use for the site, so preventing the area falling into decay and disuse which would lower the value of the land. His budget for the three years is less than the developers have spent on the model of the building they are going to put up. But from it he has created a temporary Christmas village, bright with lights and surrounded by a flowering of small craft shops. Behind this, in the old market hall, there is a makeshift roller skating rink and courts for badminton, football and other sports. The space is filled with employees from the nearby City offices at Bishopsgate and the residents of Bethnal Green. This temporary development has maintained life in the old Spitalfields Market area and kept it functioning as a bridge between the disparate communities of the City and the East End, who would otherwise have been separated by a derelict and vandalised wasteland.

Michael tells me that, with property prices dropping, many sites are now being left empty, to become eyesores which blight the surrounding area. With imaginative temporary space development and management, they can be kept in use and provide valuable community resources.

Then off to Brick Lane, the biggest exercise in 'planning for real' mounted by CLAWS. For centuries Brick Lane has provided successive waves of immigrants with their first home and place of work on British soil, before moving on elsewhere. It was here that the Jewish immigrants settled in Elizabeth I's time, receiving her personal protection. The Huguenots with their weaving skills followed in the seventeenth century. Today Brick Lane is home and bazaar to the Bangladeshi community and is being re-developed by the Brick Lane Community Development Trust (CDT).

The origins of the Brick Lane CDT lie in a highly innovative scheme, instigated first by the Prince of Wales, which brought together the public and private sector (represented by Grand Metropolitan plc and the London and Edinburgh Trust) to develop the area. Michael had been involved in the experiment as what he calls a 'bare-foot planner'. In the end, the first attempt failed because of the collapse of land prices. But the friendship struck between the Bangladeshi Community and Grand Met survived and now forms the core of the new CDT which is undertaking the redevelopment of Brick Lane under the Government's City Challenge programme. Michael had stayed on to help them. They set up models and held extensive consultation sessions with the local community, reaching, Michael estimates, about one in twenty of those who live in Brick Lane. They had to do the whole exercise in two languages, since many in the Brick Lane Bangladeshi community cannot speak English. Interpreters and dual language translations were provided.

The local Grand Met man in charge is Stewart Segal. I ask him what is in it for Grand Met. He explains that the idea first started because Sir Alan Shepherd, the Chairman of Grand Met, wanted to put something back into Brick Lane, where he was brought up. But in the process Grand Met had become convinced of the value of 'planning for real' from a commercial point of view. It enabled the developer to get a better plan and win the support of the local community, which meant that they could get their designs through the planning process quicker and with less opposition. This was worth money to them. David Brunsden, Managing Director of Grand Met Estates Ltd, in a recent speech on this kind of project, said, 'Landowners must see the commercial use in taking a medium view. Not just profit today. In today's economic climate, this approach of partnership, discussion and understanding will ultimately add value and reduce delay. I would argue that this is not altruism, it is good commercial common sense.'

It's a pity those who designed Maiden Lane didn't see it that way.

Chapter 3
'Thinking globally, acting locally.'

18 November 1992

Down to Shoreham by Sea to stay the night with Martin King, the leader of Adur District Council. I want to look at the work that Adur Council are doing on recycling waste. At 7 a.m. on a morning lashed with rain and wind, I set off with Mike Bird and Andy Christodoulou on their waste collection round along the Shoreham sea front.

◆

It has not stopped raining since we set off and the council's waterproofs have long since proved inadequate protection against this downpour driven by a lashing wind off the sea. But Andy and Mike, with whom I am working, seem impervious to the discomfort and genuinely engaged in their job. I too am rather enjoying being out in the fresh air doing something manual. But I would rather not be quite so wet.

We are working Riverside Road in Shoreham, collecting blue boxes in which the residents have put all their waste paper, glass, plastic and tins. Almost every house has a blue box outside and they are mostly full. Our job is to collect the boxes and take them to a special vehicle which Andy is driving at the moment. There, often while the lorry is still moving, we sort the rubbish into six categories, for each of which there is a separate pannier on the side of the lorry. There are three panniers for the glass; one for brown, one for green and one for clear glass. And there are other panniers for the paper, tins and plastic. When the panniers are full, their contents are lifted and emptied into bigger compartments in the body of the vehicle.

This is the first district-wide recycling collection scheme in Europe. It is the result of a three-way partnership between a consortium of twenty major international companies, together with Adur district council and West Sussex county council. It has been set up as a pilot scheme in Adur because the local council is recognised as being one of the most environmentally innovative and active, not only in Britain, but in Europe. What Mike and Andy and I are doing here could become, and many believe *should* become, the way we will all dispose of our waste and protect our environment in the future.

Last night, Martin King, who has been one of the driving forces behind Adur's environmental approach, told me, 'Adur was one of the first councils in the mid 1980s to ban the use of CFCs and hardwoods from non-sustainable sources. Our recycling centre, established in 1989, recycles a whole host of things from industrial materials, tools and spectacles [sent for reuse to the Third World] to clothes from Oxfam textile banks. We even recycle Christmas trees and wellington boots!

'To support the council's wider environmental partnership with the local community we have set up an environmental bursary which provides grants to local environmental and conservation groups from some of the proceeds gained from recycling.

'We recognise that recycling is not the complete answer to preserving our dwindling natural resources but we are doing all we can to reduce the problem. The so-called civilised world must reduce its use of non-sustainable natural resources if we are not to leave just a giant refuse tip for our grandchildren. That's why the Government is wrong to set percentage targets for recycling domestic and business waste. Each year the amount of refuse increases enormously, wasteful product packaging being one of the worst offenders. We need to reduce and reuse as well as recycle. We therefore need to measure our success against the total volume we throw away. Recycling 25 per cent of our own dustbin waste by the year 2000 [the current Government target] will be of little value if we are throwing away three times more than we do now. But even so, we could be recycling much more of what we currently throw away. Britain produces twenty million tons of household waste every year. In Adur the figure is 14,000 tons. It is calculated that half of this could be re-used and recycled. But very little is. Instead it is tipped into unsightly landfill sites. There the rubbish rots down, producing dangerous methane gas and leaching deadly pollutants into our rivers and water table. As the amount of waste we produce grows and grows, the land fill sites fill up more and more quickly and the hunt to find new ones becomes more and more difficult.

'The environmental cost of all this is hidden from us, but will be paid by our children,' Martin continued. 'But the economic cost is real and immediate. It costs £75 per tonne to collect and dispose of household refuse, making a total cost of over £150 million a year in Britain for disposing of waste, much of which we should be recycling.

'Everyone knows we cannot go on as we are, but no one knows quite how to go about changing things. What we and our partners are trying to do here is find a way to reduce costs and preserve the environment at the same time.'

The scheme they have come up with works like this:

Every householder is given a blue plastic box if they wish to have one. In this they put the four categories of recyclable waste. Where it is inappropriate to have blue boxes (for instance in blocks of flats or where the streets are too narrow for the collection vehicle), the council has issued mini recycling centres, which consist of a set of 'wheely-bins', each with a different coloured lid for the various categories of rubbish. Every week, Mike and Andy come round with their special vehicle to collect and sort the waste. Eighty-five per cent of the residents of Adur regularly participate in the scheme.

The sorted waste is then taken off to a special warehouse, where the plastic and metal is re-sorted for onward sale to the recycling companies. The newspaper is reprocessed into pulp. The steel cans are de-tinned to make the highest quality stainless steel feedstock. The aluminium and glass are melted down and re-used. The plastic is re-used for drinks bottles, plastic containers, wood substitute, plastic film, insulation, drain pipes and even flower pots. Coca-Cola in North West Europe now relies on the Adur scheme to provide the feedstock for their new recycling scheme which turns old bottles into new.

This scheme is still in its infancy. Adur is already collecting and recycling over 25 per cent of its household waste. But even this is not good enough, they say. A lot of organic household rubbish is still going to waste. So the council has offered all its residents the chance to have a 'home composter'. This consists of an odour-free plastic bin in which live a colony of tiger worms. They voraciously consume all household organic waste and swiftly turn it into the very best garden compost and liquid fertiliser.

No one has yet calculated the environmental benefit of all this. But the economic cost is greater than just collecting and dumping the waste. After the recycled materials have been sold, the net economic cost to the citizens of Adur is, Martin King calculates, 2 pence per household per day – or around £7 per year.

But the people of Adur seem quite prepared to pay the extra cost. Martin tells me that he has not received a single complaint from residents about the cost – the most common complaint is from those who feel they have been left out of the scheme.

Mike and Andy tell the same story as we work on the wind and rainswept seafront, collecting and sorting the rubbish. Andy says 'I was really amazed. I used to be an HGV driver. But I lost my job. I took this because it was the only job available but I didn't think it would work. But people seem to be really keen to do their bit. And I have become proud of the work I do – it's a bit like being a postman. He brings valuable things to the door and I take valuable things away. The people round here treat us both as doing a job that they want done.'

As I collect a box from outside one of the bungalows on Ferry Road, a man looks out of his window and recognises me, despite the council waterproofs and the fact that I must look like a drowned rat. We have a chat, sheltering in his porch out of the rain and the wind. I tell him that I am amazed at how much the residents themselves are doing to make the scheme work. He replies, 'The council's made the effort, its up to us to make the effort as well. I heard Jonathan Porritt saying the other day on

TV that if we are to protect the environment, we will have to think globally, but act locally – well that's what we are doing.'

Mike tells me that he thinks that politicians don't understand how much people want to do things that are right, not just those that are economic. Its an interesting thought to take back to the House of Commons on a blustery and rainsoaked day.

———————

Chapter 4
'She's bright, but she could be brighter.'

23 November 1992

To Shaw House Comprehensive School, in Newbury. In the evening, to a meeting of the West Berkshire Education Business Partnership, a consortium of local business people and teachers.

◆

'Here is where a Roundhead musket ball embedded itself in the wall. It narrowly missed King Charles I's head as he stood at this window in 1644, watching the battle of Newbury in the grounds below.' Mike Macleod, headteacher of Shaw House School, and I are standing in a derelict upstairs room of Shaw House, a splendid red brick Elizabethan mansion built by a wealthy Newbury cloth-merchant about 400 years ago. When, in 1943, Shaw House School's previous building in Newbury was bombed, the pupils were moved here. But they are no longer allowed in the building, which is now empty. As I look out of the window at which King Charles stood, I can see Mike's school as it is now – a collection of classrooms, permanent and temporary, clustered like besieging troops around the old building.

The culprit this time is not the Roundheads, but Berkshire County Council. In 1984 someone spotted a crack in one of the roof beams. The council was called in. They tore off all the Jacobean oak panelling searching for more cracks. They didn't find any. The cost of repairing the initial cracked beam was £10,000. But the cost of putting back the panelling they had torn off and repairing the damage they had done looking for cracks that didn't exist now amounts to £2,000,000; which of course the council cannot afford.

And so this splendid house has lain empty for nearly ten years, while the pupils and staff who could be using it crowd into inadequate 'temporary' huts which are now the Shaw House School's semi-permanent home.

But whatever the inadequacy of its buildings, this is a good school and you know it as soon as you walk through the front door. The teachers are committed and the pupils bright and engaged. The parents believe in it and support it through active governors and generous fund raising by the PTA. There is an almost tangible sense of purpose and of partnership in the enterprise of learning here.

That does not mean that Shaw House is without problems. For we are now in the depth of a recession which, even here, in the middle of prosperous southern England, is biting into the lives of parents and pupils alike and creating domestic and social problems which spill over into the education of Shaw House children.

Earlier in the day I joined in a history lesson for eight- to thirteen-year-olds. Steven Lively, their history teacher, was teaching them about poverty in England over the last 500 years. He had broken the class into groups to act out the problems of poverty in each century. His pupils had thrown themselves into the lesson with a will, one group even drawing me into their play about the poor law. After the lesson, I asked how many in the class had a member of their family who was unemployed. Around 80 per cent raised their hands. And every single child put their hands up when I asked how many had a friend or relative out of work.

Afterwards, at a tutor's meeting with John Martin, the head of year two, I heard more about the human effects of the current recession. We discussed what could be done for one bright young fifteen-year-old, who had become aggressive and almost unteachable after his father had been made unemployed and his family's house re-possessed. I was told that teachers are having to spend more and more time picking up the pieces as families break up under the strain of unemployment, house re-possessions and business bankruptcies.

The economic situation is also having an effect on the broader aspects of education. More pupils are having difficulties with buying school uniform and fewer are able to afford school trips and the equipment to take part in outside-school activities.

But the unemployment situation has had one good side-effect. Sixty per cent of Shaw House pupils are now going on to further education, twice as many as a few years ago. It is easy to see why. In the past when jobs were plentiful, the financial reward of leaving school at sixteen and getting a job was much more attractive than staying in further education. But all that had changed. Of those who had left Shaw House at sixteen over the last three years, two hundred were known to be still unemployed.

Drugs, even here in Newbury, are becoming an increasing problem, too. There was a case recently where one ex-pupil had died of an overdose. There is some suspicion that drug trafficking may even have reached the margins of the school, but this had been investigated and found to be untrue. But they had had to deal with a brief incident of solvent abuse recently.

To add to the uncertainties and domestic pressures caused by the recession, there is the disruption caused by constant changes in Government education policies.

One of the teachers put it to me graphically. 'See that fifteen year old,' he said. 'She's bright. But she could be brighter. There has been not one year in her education when she and those who have taught her have not had to cope with the imposition of major change to the way she has been taught.'

Not that most teachers I spoke to think that all the changes have, in themselves, been bad. Most of them are welcomed. The national curriculum was necessary, even it it is now too inflexible; giving schools control of their own budget was good, even if some schools and their governors use the freedom it gives them to hire the cheapest rather than the best teachers. And testing is right, if only the Government had chosen a method which helped pupils and measured the real quality of schools. But, however good the changes, the way they have been imposed has been disruptive to the pupils. There has been no consultation with teachers, no warning, no pilot testing and no time to prepare. The changes have simply been imposed, either through legislation from the House of Commons, or through edicts handed down by the Government. Often they have been reversed or changed a year later.

Teachers, I was told, can cope with falling resources and bad accommodation. In the end they will overcome both in order to provide the education they believe their pupils deserve. But the constant changes imposed from the top, and the Government's continual attacks on the teaching profession which have accompanied them, has undermined morale. John Martin said 'If you're good and you're young in my profession, you are probably looking for a chance to leave it.'

There was much criticism of the newly imposed testing system. The tests had been brought in too late for the teachers to prepare their pupils and many children would be unfairly judged as a result. And they were time consuming, bureaucratic and designed not to encourage children by emphasising strengths and helping overcome weaknesses, but to divide them into successes and failures. Tests like this would encourage teachers to 'teach to test', concentrating on giving children the ability to pass exams on a given June afternoon, at the cost of a broader education which would help them throughout their lives. Perhaps worst of all, publication of test results in their 'raw' state would, I was told, result in unfair judgements being made about schools. Those schools which served middle-class areas, like Shaw House, would always have better results than those in more deprived catchments. One teacher said that what most tests would show was not the quality of the teaching, but the social make-up of the area. The result would be a two-tier education, with better schools in the middle-class areas and 'sink' schools in the poorer ones. If test results are to be published and put in league tables so that parents can know the quality of their local schools, then allowance must be made for the social mix of the area so that the education 'value added' for each school can be properly assessed.

Mike showed me round his school administration system. He

welcomed the fact that Shaw House now had control of its own budget. It reduced interference from Shire Hall and gave them the flexibility to do the things they wanted to with the money they had available. He was lucky; he had excellent governors and an active parents' body. But he knew of some schools in poorer areas which could not rely on parents' support and had great difficulty finding anyone to act as a governor. He was also very critical of what he described as the 'market-based' education system, which pitted one school in direct market competition for pupils with its neighbour. He believed that many schools were now being forced to spend more of their limited resources promoting their schools through brochures and marketing techniques, than they were on raising educational standards. He said that the effect of this could well be that one of Newbury's schools might have to close as a result of the financial pressure.

And the present system is still far too bureaucratic and inflexible. When Shaw House and the other Berkshire schools were given control of their own budgets, a group of mathematics teachers had gone through the figures with a fine-tooth comb. They found that a mistake had been made which cost schools like Shaw House £20,000 per year. They complained to the county, who accepted the error and agreed that the schools had lost out. But in the meantime, Berkshire had been 'rate capped' by the Government, limiting the amount of money they could spend. So the underpayment could not be recovered, either in that year or any subsequent one. They had, in effect, lost the money for good.

After school, Mike takes me to visit the West Berkshire Partnership, a local educational organisation, made up of the heads of all the local schools, representatives from the county council education and careers authorities and a number of the key industrialists and businessmen in the area. They meet at 6.30p.m. in Newbury. Present are businessmen and women from a marketing firm, a computer firm selling software to the Japanese, the local gas board and about ten other Newbury businesses. There are not many small business representatives – and I notice that there are more teachers at this meeting than industrialists.

The Partnership was originally set up using part funding provided by the Government and has done a lot to bring industry and business together: helping local schools to deliver the national curriculum, establishing a record of achievement system for pupils doing work experience at local firms, planning initiatives to help the young unemployed and assisting local schools to match the skills they teach with the needs of business in the area. One of the headteachers present tells me that this partnership with business has already had a considerable influence on teaching practice and culture in the area.

The scheme was so successful that local firms willingly contributed to its running costs. But the Government made it impossible to plan ahead by refusing to tell the Partnership what funds they would have for the financial year, beginning each April, until the end of that month! Now they have been told that the core funding provided by the Government will be completely withdrawn in 1994. As we sit in the conference room at Bayer House, the headquarters of Bayer plc, the multi-national chemical firm, there is real fear expressed by teachers and businessmen alike that they may not be able to keep the operation going. One of the businessmen tells me 'I think that for the Government this is just a gimmick to take the pressure off them on unemployment. They are not treating it seriously, which is a pity because it really is doing some good and business does want to take education seriously. Most of us realise that good, relevant education is essential if our businesses are to succeed.'

Donald Lee, Bayer's company pharmacist, who chairs the Partnership, adds, 'The Government seems to think that local firms will fund it, but just at the moment most local firms are having enough of a hard time funding themselves. I fear it will fold in a year or so, more's the pity. A lot will be lost if it goes. One of our main problems has been the duplication of Government agencies we have to deal with. We have an alphabet soup of Government schemes and bodies and no one really knows who does what. There is a lot of overlap and waste. We need a single body which represents business, organises and co-ordinates training and has the power to take action. On the Continent, in France and Germany, their chambers of commerce do this. Here chambers are not recognised by the Government in the same way. We could do better and waste less if we learnt from the Continental experience.'

I ask him what he, as a major employer in a successful industry, would like to see out of our education system. He replies: 'I think we are placing far too much emphasis on specialisation. We are in a time of very fast-moving change. What I want is a good grounding in the basics, a broad range of knowledge and the ability to learn. The national curriculum is a good idea in principle, but it's far too narrow and far too inflexible.'

As I drive to London after the meeting I reflect that, whatever its problems, I have been in a good school in a prosperous town which has the interest and the people and the resources to support their children in their education years.

Chapter 5

'Michael – gifted? Surely you don't mean Michael Dadze?'

24 November 1992

To Peckham, where I spend the night of 24 November and, on the following day, visit the Dadze family who live on the North Camden estate. I spend much of the rest of the day in a local school, talking to teachers and joining in their classes.

◆

We are sitting in Joanna and Kwame Dadze's flat on the North Camden estate in Peckham, South London. Joanna and Kwame have lived here for nine years. On the first Christmas they were here, Joanna found a dead body lying outside. No one had paid much notice. They had seen others since.

Next door is a flat which has been burnt out. I have already noticed many others on the estate. Joanna tells me that some are the result of petrol bombs being put through the door, but most have been started by tenants who are so desperate to leave the estate that they burn their own flats in the hope that the council will re-house them elsewhere.

Joanna says that she never lets her children out unsupervised, even during daylight; it's just too dangerous. On my way here I saw why. In the dark underground garages beneath the flats, in the corners of stairwells and in the recesses of the walkways is the rubbish of the drug culture which flourishes here: discarded needles, disused 'crack pipes', the left overs and left behinds of last night's drug-induced degradation.

After dark, these spaces are the domain of drug users and pushers. On dark winter evenings, local children from the age of six have to walk through them on their way home from school. You can't escape drugs in this area, no matter how young you are.

Kwame and Joanna's flat is bare, but scrupulously clean. The television is on in the corner as we talk. There is an old hi-fi in another corner. We sit on a derelict sofa which will have had many previous owners. In the room are two other chairs, a table, a spill of children's books, a few well-used toys and two of the Dadze children, Michael and Andrew. The third, three-year-old Kwase, is in bed.

Kwame and Joanna are Ghanaians. He is a catering worker and earns £125 per week. He has spent a good deal of time away from the family, as many Ghanaian men do. And as in most Ghanaian families, it is the woman who holds the family together and makes it work.

Joanna Dadze is woman of immediate and impressive dignity. She looks horribly tired, but behind her exhausted face shines a strong and determined personality whose whole force is given to her children. When Kwame was away, the family had to do without his wage. So Joanna had worked all night and looked after her family during the day. Now he is back, things are easier.

Now she starts work at 2a.m. each morning as a 'self-employed' contract office cleaner in Fleet Street. When she finishes there, she moves on to clean the offices of banks and building societies in the City. She returns home at 7.30a.m. and, wheeling the baby, takes her children to school. She doesn't send Andrew to the nearest school, because there is another one rather further away which she thinks is better. Then back home to look after the baby, clean her home and cook the meals, before going back to pick up Michael and Andrew after school. She will not let her children walk to or from school alone. She cat-naps as she can throughout the day.

The money she earns goes towards the £400 per term necessary to top up the 75 per cent scholarship her son Michael receives to attend a private school for gifted children. Michael, who is now eight years old, taught himself to read at the age of three. No one saw him do it or knows how it happened. Joanna says that he started by reading the junk mail that came through their door and, since he first crawled, he has never had a book out of his hand. He began playing with computers at three. He was taught to count to nineteen and was then able, instinctively, to carry on to a thousand.

But school was a disaster for Michael. At the age of five he went to a local infants school, but was bored and became difficult and withdrawn. The class teacher, trying desperately to cope with a multi-lingual, multi-ethnic class of thirty, saw Michael as a problem child, not a gifted one. By chance, Joanna knew a local woman, Cherry, who worked on a voluntary basis with local schools assisting children with learning difficulties, and turned to her for help. At first, Cherry thought Michael might be autistic. But, having the time to spend with him, she soon identified Michael's extraordinary gifts. Cherry advised Joanna to contact the National Association for Gifted Children. But Joanna couldn't cope with the forms. Eventually Cherry and Joanna went to see the school authorities.

The first teacher they saw told them that she followed a policy of 'class equalisation', which meant that all children were to be treated exactly the same. That applied to colour, religion, class and race – and it applied to ability, too. She was not prepared to treat Michael as exceptional.

So Joanna and Cherry went to see the head to ask for an IQ test. They explained that Michael was exceptionally gifted. The reply was 'Gifted – Michael? Surely you don't mean Michael Dadze, do you? Of course he isn't.' When, finally, they tested

Michael, he scored a verbal scale of 141, putting him in the top 0.3 per cent of the population.

Joanna tells me that she would probably have given up had it not been for Cherry – after all who was Joanna to say that she was right and all these experts and authorities had got it wrong? But they were forced to listen to Cherry because she was educated and because she was white. So together they had persisted and now Michael had won the scholarship to a school for specially gifted children. Cherry later told me that the Dadze's third child, Kwase, maybe even more gifted than Michael. But this time, after Michael, it won't be so difficult.

Earlier in the day I went to see one of the local schools. It was not difficult to see why, in schools like this, Michael's abilities had been missed.

The school building, which houses both an infants and a junior school, is an old Victorian one. Solidly built and imposing amongst the meaner houses which surround it, it would, in its day, have made a statement about the importance of education. Today these two schools are testimony to an education system which is weakened by underfunding and crumbling under the weight of the social problems.

The staff tell me that inner London schools like this one are becoming so submerged in social problems that they are able to devote less and less time to teaching. About half the pupils at the school do not have English as a first language. The only way for the different ethnic groups to survive in this area is to stick together. So polarisation between racial groups and ethnic solidarity within them is often not so much a proud expression of race, as a practical means for survival.

One teacher told me that there was no interest among parents in running the school – but there was a lot of interest in the education of their own children. They would spend their last pennies dressing their children smartly. 'If only we spent more time teaching parents how to participate in their children's education and less effort persuading them to run schools, we might be getting somewhere.'

Drugs, so openly available in the area, cannot be kept off the school site. A child had recently been caught selling drugs in the junior school, which takes pupils up to the age of eleven.

But drugs were not thought yet to have reached the infants school. And along with the drugs has come increasing violence, both on the playground and toward the teachers.

But even where drugs are not available, their influence is still felt. Carol Green, the head of the infants school, told me of a five-year-old who had been persistently left alone on the school site after 3.30p.m. Teachers had agreed a rota to stay behind and to look after her till she was picked up. If, by 6p.m., the mother had still not appeared, social services were contacted, and they either re-united the child with her mother, a confirmed drug addict, or found her a place for the night. Concerned about the welfare of the child, the school had begged social services to do something more permanent. But they too are under pressure. Nothing had been done until, eventually, the mother had been arrested by the police for theft. Then the authorities finally acted and made new arrangements.

Carol, like all the staff I met at the school, is a dedicated and gifted teacher with a strong sense of commitment both to her profession and to the area. She tells me that this area had always had its difficulties, but now things are getting steadily worse. The school is having to pick up the problems from the increase in family breakdowns. She sees television as a contributory factor. Not just because of screen violence, but more because watching TV all day erodes the communication skills without which learning is impossible. This is particularly so, she believes, in cases where TV provides a compelling form of access to our culture and language for children in whose home no English is spoken.

Indeed language is itself the biggest single problem these two schools have to cope with. In Carol's current reception class, for children just coming to the school, there are two children who have no English at all. In last September's intake, half of the children had English only as a second language. Including Nigerian and Ghanaian dialects, the breakdown of the first languages of pupils from new-Commonwealth countries was as follows (numbers of pupils in brackets): Estaki(1), Efic(1), Ebo(1), Yoruba(16), Wolof(1), Bengali(3), Twi(1), Punjabi(2), Ikwerne(1), Bendel(1), Vernacular Ghanaian(3), Hausa(1), Katchi(1), Khana(1). In addition there were, from non-Commonwealth countries: Cypriot Turkish(6), Cantonese(4), Vietnamese(2), Russian(1), Portuguese(1), Spanish(1), Arabic(2) and Kurdish(1). The Government gives grants to help with the education of new-Commonwealth pupils, but, for the others, the local education authority and the school picks up the bill. 'How do I begin to teach the national curriculum with these kind of problems to cope with?' Carol says despairingly.

The whole procedure for helping children with learning difficulties has also clearly broken down in this part of south London because there are not the resources to back it up. Under the present system, a child with learning difficulties has an assessment and then special facilities are designed to meet their needs. This is done through a 'statement' listing the child's problem and what must be done about it.

But in this inner city area, the number of children with learning difficulties runs far ahead of the funding available. So a child with learning difficulties can start the process of 'statementing' in their first year of school, but not have their 'statement' issued until half way through their school career. By which time, of course, it is almost always too late.

And the lack of resources to cope with the special problems of inner city schools like this one is not only blighting children socially. It is also placing them at a huge educational disadvantage to those in more fortunate areas. One teacher told me that a 'statemented' child who had recently come from a Home Counties school was said to be in need of special education facilities because he had learning difficulties. In this school he easily fitted in at about the mid-point of the ability range.

I see what all this means in practice when I join Sadie Jones, who is giving a lesson in geometrical shapes to ten-year-olds as part of the national maths curriculum. There were more than thirty in her class. Ethnic and religious groups I was able to identify included Rastafarians, Chinese, Arabs and Somalis. Sadie, herself of mixed race, is an experienced and dedicated teacher. But I can sense her anxiety and anxiousness at her inability to fulfil her own professional aspirations and teach to the standards she believes in, given the impossible conditions she has to cope with. Her class contains the full ability range across two years of entry. There are children here who cannot read and who cannot express themselves effectively. Amongst the various ethnic groups, many had insufficient basic English to benefit from the lesson. After the lesson was over, Sadie showed me the complex and voluminous forms the Government's new assessment scheme now requires her to fill in for each pupil. In classes of the size and nature they are having to cope with here, it is almost impossible to fill them in accurately. 'Frankly its a pretty hit and miss affair. The best I can do in assessing most of these children is make an inspired guess. I wish someone from the government had come down here and looked at what their forms mean in practice in a class like this.' If there is another Michael Dadze here, it would be pure luck that he would ever be discovered.

Later, in the staff room one teacher told me that multiple deprivation and poverty are often accompanied by high levels of child abuse. In an average class of thirty in the school there would probably be two or three who had suffered abuse. By the time children left school at the age of eleven, perhaps as many as ten per cent would have experienced abuse of some sort or another.

Another said to me 'The problem is, the raw material is getting worse and worse – I know its not very "politically correct" to say that, but I can't think of another way of putting it. The social problems, the drugs, the rise in crime; in the end it's just swamping us and no matter how well we try to teach, we are losing ground the whole time. I hate to think what problems we are causing for the future. If a child has literacy problems, or finds it difficult to keep up, they just have to be left behind, while the teacher takes the rest of the class on. We in this school are lucky enough to have Cherry, who has given her time to the school to help those who have learning difficulties. Were it not for her, these children would be permanently left behind and effectively cut out of any further benefit from the education system. In most other schools, I suspect that is what happens to them.'

I spend some time with Cherry, a remarkable woman who gives much of her time to the school and has now become the last hope for these lost children. She is the only permanent resource they have to help with children who have difficulties with literacy. She and her husband have chosen to live in Peckham because they are determined to do what is personally possible to stop the rot in areas like this.

Cherry is a largely self taught, but she is an outstanding and deeply patient teacher. Her pupils that day, two children of African origin, had been sent to her because of language and reading problems. The lesson I attend consists of phonetics and literacy games. I watch the children, even in one lesson, respond to the individual attention which the school cannot otherwise provide for them. Cherry told me that some of her pupils are so withdrawn that she often has to spend days just to get them to make eye contact with her. She told me of one recent pupil who she had tried, but failed, to help. She simply couldn't reach him. He seemed to have absolutely no sense of morality or order. She had found him very frightening and in desperate need of access to help from an educational psychologist. But none was available.

I left impressed at the dedication of the teachers I had met, angry at the waste of human talent in an education system which is so underfunded that it is manifestly failing the people it is supposed to serve and deeply concerned about the problems we are storing up with children who have learnt very early that, for them, there is no way out.

Chapter 6
'A chance to hope again'

24 November 1992

To Camden to visit the Camden Training Centre for unemployed in North London.

◆

'The aim of this place,' Ian Roe tells me, 'is to give those who have lost hope of getting a job, a chance to hope again.'

Ian is the director of the Camden Training Centre in North London. Here they run vocational training and adult education courses for the left out and the left behind; some have such a low opinion of themselves that they will not even apply for training because they do not think they are good enough. Outreach workers from the centre have to go out into the ethnic minority communities to find and persuade people to apply to the centre for training. Most difficult are women from some ethnic minority groups, where the culture is opposed to women working and the opinions and hostility of husbands have to be overcome.

Ian tells me as we walk round that the centre operates on the basis of fixed quotas for ethnic minority and women students. There are also courses exclusively for women. But, in addition, every mixed gender course has a target figure of at least 50 per cent women, 40 per cent from the black ethnic minority communities and 8 per cent from amongst people with disabilities. 'Quotas are a kind of self-imposed discipline on our work,' Ian explains 'Without them, all our courses would be taken up by the middle class and the whites and those aren't the people we want to get at. Our job is to reach those who would otherwise be left out.'

We visit classes in painting, decorating, plumbing, carpentry, computers, electronics, typing and basic literacy. The Camden Training Centre, regarded by many as a pioneer in work with inner city unemployed from disadvantaged groups, has a turn-over of £1.2 million per year. Forty per cent of this comes from Camden council. The rest comes from London Training and Enterprise Councils (TECs) and the European Social Fund (ESF). There is additional support from the private sector.

ESF funds run from January to December, whereas British practice, followed by local and national government alike, budgets for a year which runs from April to March. This makes life complicated.

But it is the Department of Environment (DOE) which makes it almost impossible. The centre had to bid to the DOE for funds through a horrendously complicated process. Even after the money has been agreed for a given year (usually months after the year had actually started), it takes ages to come through, creating considerable difficulties with cash flow. In 1991, they were still waiting for funds allocated in 1989 to be paid. This meant that the centre was often forced to sail dangerously close to technical breach of trading and insolvency laws.

Camden Council helps the centre out by lending them money to cover the gap. But they charge 11 per cent interest – which means that more than 10 per cent of the money the Government gives to fund training for some of the most deprived in London is wasted because the DOE cannot get its act together.

Ian tells me that at one point in 1992 more than £8 million pounds was still outstanding to voluntary organisations in London as a result of delayed payments by the Government. This forced some voluntary training and welfare organisations who rely on these funds for their work to close down. 'Voluntary organisations offer the Government an efficient and very cost-effective way of reaching those whom Government schemes will not reach – but sheer inefficiency and bureaucracy is now putting them out of business,' Ian tells me.

And the lack of co-ordination does not stop there. Trainees who start a Government scheme for the unemployed receive a supplement of £10 on their welfare benefit. But trainees on courses funded by the ESF do not qualify for benefit, and are deemed to be 'in remunerative work'. So the Government does not pay these students unemployment benefit; but it does exclude them from the numbers of the unemployed. On top of this trainees on ESF-funded courses who receive a 'training allowance' lose a proportion of their income support and have their entitlement to other benefits reduced.

Ian explains that this is an absurd anomaly, since both programmes are targeted towards the same people (the unemployed) and since the Government itself receives a substantial percentage of the costs of its own training programme from the ESF.

Courses at the centre are open to anyone. No educational qualifications are required and there is no pre-selection. They recently came under pressure from Camden council (of whom Ian speaks very highly) to introduce entry qualifications and pre-selection. The council claimed these would reduce course drop-outs and wastage. The centre agreed to do a trial competition with the local Further Education College, who require educational qualification and run a strenuous pre-selection system.

At the end of the period, the centre got a pass rate double that of the college. The secret, Ian tells me, is to take a holistic approach to students' needs. The centre has an efficient Training Support Services Section which deals with welfare, houses homeless students and acts as their advocate with the local authorities and the welfare system. The centre also provides a full package of child care. 'Without child care,' Mitzi Rampersad, who heads the Support Services Section tells me, 'the women we get here could never come. They would remain trapped in their homes.'

And without accommodation, single, homeless men, like Abi, a young black man I later spoke to, would be left out as well. Abi had lived for most of the period of his training in a hostel the centre had found for him. 'But what will I do after my year's training is over?' Abi asks.

That is the question on the lips of all the trainees I speak to. One articulate young black man, learning plumbing and absorbed in it, tells me that he was on the edge of taking up a criminal life style when he had been persuaded to come to the centre for training. He decided that he had nothing to lose, so he might as well give it a try. 'This has given me dignity and a new chance – but what happens at the end when I am trained and there still isn't a job to go to? My woman thinks this is a ticket to heaven and riches, but I think I will just end up where I was before.'

I spend some time chatting to a group of trainees who are qualifying as decorators. They are mostly black and proud of their new skills. Many want to go self-employed, but they are discouraged by the sudden and painful loss of welfare they would suffer. What they want is a system of welfare which would encourage job flexibility and self-employment by gradually withdrawing benefit as their businesses grew.

As I leave, Ian says 'I believe that everyone has the potential to achieve if the training process is properly resourced. The main objective of the centre is to provide access to recognised vocational qualifications and to give people a route into employment. Our aim is to equip people with the necessary skills and confidence to make their own decisions about what they do with their own lives.'

Chapter 7
'People with good jobs don't live here.'

25 November 1992

To the Industrial Society in Farringdon, London, where I meet with Oliver Johnston, their national campaign leader, and his staff. Then to Safeway's new store in Wapping to meet those working there.

◆

'I had given up hope of ever having a job again, and now, here I am in charge of the whole frozen food section – I shall be a manager soon.'

Charles is in his mid twenties, of African origin and lives in

London's East End. He has a cheerful, intelligent face and is, for the first time in his life, in a job and clearly proud of what he does.

He is one of forty local people who applied for jobs in the new Safeways store in Wapping in 1992. They were all long-term unemployed and most had never worked or even had a job interview in their lives. Safeway had called in Oliver Johnston and his team from the Industrial Society to help recruit people from the local community for their new store. From the original forty, fifteen had been chosen for a two day 'pre-selection' course run by the Industrial Society and attended by Safeways managers. The aim of the course was to give the fifteen sufficient self confidence and interview skills to be able to apply for the Safeways vacancies on an equal basis with other applicants. After the course, they went through the formal interview with Safeways and nine, including Charles, were finally offered employment.

Earlier, in the Industrial Society's London offices in Farringdon, Oliver Johnston and his colleagues – Gail Greengross, Area Project Co-ordinator, and Darren Barlow, their Management Adviser – had explained to me why it was necessary to go through such a long process in order to find Safeways an employee and Charles a job. Oliver started by telling me what his team did.

'The Industrial Society moved into projects to help the long-term unemployed in 1986, when the Government set up their inner-city task forces. Our job was to find out how to reach the long-term unemployed and set up schemes to bring them back into the labour market. We soon realised what a difficult job this was. Many have been out of work so long that they have become, in effect, unemployable. They don't wait to be rejected by employers, they reject themselves by not applying for the jobs in the first place. They have been turned down so many times that they have basically given up.

'Our first job is to find these people in the communities in which they live. Then we try to help them regain their self confidence. Then we have to teach them how to apply for jobs and what to do at interviews. Only then can we consider persuading them to apply for vacancies. We deal chiefly with twenty-three to twenty-six-year-olds – those who were unemployed in the last recession and have been unemployed ever since. Most have never worked. We give those who come to us the kind of attention and quality of training which most firms would only give to management trainees.'

Gail tells me that when they were first established in North Peckham the Industrial Society advertised training courses linked to jobs north of the river, but had not a single response. They discovered that people in Peckham often do not apply for jobs north of the river, because they do not think themselves good enough. So Gail had to change her tactics. Instead of waiting for the unemployed to come to her, she went out to find them. She went to community meetings, drop-in centres for the unemployed, benefit offices – she even distributed leaflets through people's doors. She explained that one of the best ways to make contact with the ethnic minority communities of East London was through 'Saturday schools'. These, like the 350 strong Indo-Chinese Saturday school in Lewisham, enable ethnic minority groups to socialise, teach their religion, preserve their language and culture and supplement mainstream education. Gail had at once time or another visited all fifteen of the Saturday schools in South London in order to reach the young unemployed from minority ethnic backgrounds who she was trying to bring back into work.

The Industrial Society also works with large employers, many of the most enlightened of whom, like Safeways, actively seek local people as employees. I ask Oliver why they did this; why not choose from the better 'raw material' which was available from less deprived areas of London?

He replies, 'Many employers, particularly in the retail industry, believe it is commercially valuable to them to match their staff to their customers. Like Safeways in Wapping, they want to be seen by the community to be in favour of providing jobs for the community, not only because they see this as the right thing to do. It also encourages the community to shop with them. Sometimes, failing to get the right mix of staff can damage sales. A leading chain of record stores, for instance, advertised for staff and took what they thought to be the best available. Only afterwards did they discover that the middle-class graduates who staffed their stores did not have the same musical tastes as their customers. So their staff played the wrong sort of music in their shops and were ignorant of the music their customers wanted. We helped them to get staff more suited to their customer base. The ultimate in this philosophy is Anita Roddick's Body Shop, where a close relationship between the ethos and background of the staff and that of their customers is one of the shop's main selling points. And a very good thing too – since it gives locals the chance of a job they would never otherwise have.

'Of course, it still more often works the other way. The jobs created on many new "green field" sites, especially in some of the new car factories, seem to be filled almost exclusively from outside the communities in which they are set up.'

As with the Camden Centre, Oliver and Gail stress the need to have a holistic approach to their people. They often have to persuade employers setting up in a deprived area that to get young local employees they will have to set up crèche and child-care facilities and support housing intiatives for local single young people.

Gail explains that the Government set a three-year time limit on the Industrial Society's contracts to launch employment initiatives in deprived areas. After that, the community projects they set up have to stand on their own feet. She doubts if they can – many will simply fold up.

'What we are actually doing,' Gail explained, 'is not just getting people back to work, but also helping communities to regain their self respect. Long years of neglect and unemployment have not only damaged personal self-regard, they have also destroyed community cohesion. Deprivation and failure becomes increasingly accepted as the natural condition and even celebrated as a means of identification. The Craigmillar area just outside Edinburgh is a typical example of what can happen. The Craigmillar community still struggles to free itself from the label of a "slum clearance" estate, even though the slum clearance took place over fifty years ago. Its "bad" reputation has had the effect of setting up barriers to employment – so-called "post code discrimination". Local people lose confidence and present themselves poorly for interview, creating a situation where poor self regard feeds poor reputation in a vicious downward spiral. After a while, the community begins to take a certain perverse pride in its poor image. This, together with a long-standing and active Labour

Party tradition often seem to be the primary forces for social cohesion in the Craigmillar community. If you took these away, Craigmillar would lose its identity. If you live in Craigmillar and are lucky enough to get a good job, people expect you to move away. "People with good jobs don't live here" – that's the Craig-millar attitude. Things are improving in Craigmillar now, but it has taken a combined initiative from the community, statutory bodies and the private sector, backed by the input of substantial funds to break out of the spiral.'

Gail continues: 'If you threaten a middle-class community, say by putting a motorway through the middle, the community will automatically come together and leaders and organisations will naturally emerge to fight their corner. In most of the communities we work with, such a sense of cohesion and confidence died years ago, though the remnants can often still be found. In Lewisham we found more than fifty voluntary organisations working with and for the unemployed. Our first job was to bring them together. The next problem is that, if we succeed, we create a "community free-market", successful communities begin to compete with each other over very minimal resources and diminishing opportunities. But at least this is better than the apathy which we find when we start.

'Then there is the problem of the personal challenge of work. For many in their mid twenties who have never had a job, getting one is a traumatic experience. For the first time in their lives they have to leave the peer group which has been the only circle of contact they have known, as children, in school and on the dole. Adjusting to the new peer group at work can be a very difficult experience. If we are really serious about finding jobs for the long-term unemployed in this left-out generation, we need to recognise that the problem is much bigger than merely finding them jobs.'

Oliver goes on to tell me about the shifting nature of work. 'Whether we like it or not, part-time work is becoming more and more a fact of life. In future we will have increasingly flexible jobs. Many people are already making their living through a 'portfolio' of part-time jobs. Only the minority will work fixed 9-to-5 hours in a secure career structure that lasts from their teens to sixty-five. Most will have shifting and fractured patterns of employment, some part and some full time, at different times in their lives. We will have to change our welfare systems so that they accommodate and encourage flexibility, rather than penalise those who work unconventional or flexible work patterns, as at present. And we will have to think of new ways to protect workers' rights. Fractured work means fractured collective power in the work place. If we are not careful the power of those who employ will become too great – perhaps it already is becoming too great. Already the opportunities for exploitation are worrying and some unscrupulous employers are taking advantage of the weakness of part-time labour. If we are to protect the rights of those at work it will have to be done through laws which protect individual rights, including those of part-time workers, rather than by relying on the collective power of the unions.'

I recall my own two periods of unemployment and remember how it affected me after only six months without a job. The underlying levels of unemployment seem set to rise and rise. More and more people will be semi-permanently excluded from the personal dignity which, in our society, comes only through having a job. In the force of these changes, maintaining our social cohesion and even stability, and giving chances to people like Charles, will depend on our ability to find new ways to arrange and distribute available work and to give those who are left out the kind of support they need to get back in. Oliver, Gail and their colleagues at the Industrial Society are beginning to find new ways to approach this huge problem for the future.

———————

Chapter 8

'We are allowed to keep people alive here by giving them food; but we're not allowed to stop them being killed by shells and bullets.'

12–17 December 1992

By RAF aircraft to Split and then up by road through central Bosnia to visit British troops and aid workers, through to Sarajevo, across the front line to the Bosnian Serb headquarters at Pale, returning through Sarajevo, central Bosnia and Zagreb to Britain.

◆

It is said that the British Royal Engineer, Lieutenant Colonel John Field, purchased this twenty-five-mile road across the Dinaric Alps in central Bosnia from the local Croats a few months ago, paying, on behalf of the British taxpayer, the princely sum of 10 dinars – slightly less than 1 penny. In my view he paid too much. To call it a road would be an exaggeration – a miserable little dirt track would be as far as any reasonable person might be prepared to go. But up it, thanks to the miracles performed by British Royal Engineers, passes much of the vital aid which keeps the beleaguered population of Central Bosnia alive and every food ration, spare part and round of ammunition which keeps the British Army there operational and able to do its job. Across it, now that it is open, also travel many local vehicles, carrying farmers about their seasonal business and pitiful car loads of refugees fleeing from ethnic cleansing and the fighting further north.

At present it is snowing lightly. A thin layer of ice, covered by a light dusting of snow, makes negotiating this difficult track, running along the edge of hair-raising drops, even more dangerous. A British army truck, painted in white UN colours and carrying heavy equipment to the forward British troops twenty miles to our north, has slipped on one of the tight bends and is now balancing precariously, two wheels off the road, over the edge of a vertiginous drop. We are stuck and will be, it seems, for another two hours or so while the road is cleared.

Also caught in this Bosnian traffic jam are the flotsam and jetsam of this terrible war. There are civilian aid trucks, many driven by British volunteers who have raised money in their communities, gathered food and now risk their lives to come out here and deliver it. There are also Croat farmers carrying livestock and goods to market, more white UN lorries travelling in and out of the battle zone, two car loads of Muslim refugees going south with young children and the pathetic remains of their hitherto peaceful lives and assorted members of the world's press. All sit more or less patiently waiting for the blockage to clear, while young British soldiers, not one with a word of the local language, calmly take command of the situation and try various methods to unblock the road.

While we are waiting, I get chatting to a journalist in a neighbouring vehicle. He turns out to be an American and a military expert, who writes for *Janes' Weekly* – the world's most authoritative journal on military matters. He is out here looking at the various troops which make up the UN forces in Bosnia. He tells me, unbidden, 'I have now seen all the troops here in this polyglot force. I can tell you that this lot,' he gesticulates to a young Royal Engineer corporal moving a Croat farmer's truck full of chickens to make way for a recovery vehicle, 'this lot leave the rest absolutely standing – they take no nonsense, they are disciplined, resourceful, well equipped, well led and very, very effective. If all the UN's troops were of equivalent quality, this problem would not now be as bad as it is.'

Early this morning, long before dawn, I left Split, eighty miles to the south accompanied by Bob Regan, a civilian working for the Ministry of Defence, Corporal Matty, who is driving us, and Nick South from my office. We drove up the ascending ridges which rise like steps from the Dalmatian coast towards the Dinaric Alps. Dawn broke clear and very cold as we descended from the final ridge into the high bowl which contains the little town of Tomislavgrad, lying at the foot of the Dinaric Alps. This is home to the rear echelon troops who keep our front-line forces in Bosnia fed, supplied and operational at the end of 'route triangle', which we are now travelling, thirty miles to the east. We joined them for breakfast and then started our ascent into the snow line and past the little forest camps of Royal Engineers who made this road passable and must keep it open whatever the vicious Bosnian winter delivers in the months ahead. One local has already told me that when the snow really comes, they will not keep this road open. The local Royal Engineers captain says he will. I believe the captain.

We are free and moving again in an hour. Over the highest point in our route now, we descend into an alpine valley. There is a mountain lake below us, surrounded by neat villages and woods and peaceful farm land. It is difficult to imagine there is a war going on in the midst of such beauty. But we are soon brought back to reality as we pass through the town of Prozor. Here the Croats burnt out their Muslim neighbours a few weeks ago. There was brutality and some killing. As we pass through the little town there are houses burnt in every street; there are black-shirted Croat 'HOS' extremists at every corner – they wear Nazi-type arm bands and are well armed; there are Croat nationalist flags and there is visible hostility at our passage. If British troops can no longer do their job in Bosnia and have to withdraw, they will have to pull back through this town. It may not be easy.

Then on over more ridges and down to the rear position of the British forward unit, the B company of the First Cheshires at Gornij Vakuf. Here we get a cup of tea and a briefing on the local military situation from the young company commander. He is matter of fact and cool about what is, by any standards, a very difficult and dangerous operation. Then, as darkness falls, we press on for the First Cheshires' headquarters at Vitez, a further thirty miles to the north. More dirt tracks, hard roads and narrow gorges.

We arrive at Vitez shortly after 9p.m., after sixteen hours on the road, to be met by Colonel Bob Stewart, the commanding officer of the First Cheshires and, thanks to this war, by now a familiar face on British television screens. Over the next two days I am to spend a good deal of time with 'Colonel Bob', as he is known to his men. He is a bluff, simple and brave soldier of the sort whom, down the centuries, Britain has sent abroad to fight for the causes our politicians thought were important. He is a soldier's soldier: always at the front; never asking his men to do more than he does; always ready, when he feels it necessary, to push against the edges of the careful political lines his superiors have drawn for him from the safety of London and the rear headquarters. He is not one of those soldiers who is half politician. He can be bombastic and he is often neither careful nor diplomatic. This has not always made him popular with his superiors. But it has made him effective in the area he commands, where all three sides in this war have learnt to understand that the British troops mean business and should not be tampered with. This has meant that the UN has been far more effective in keeping the peace necessary for the safe delivery of aid in this area than in other UN sectors. And that has undoubtedly meant the difference between life and death for many of those in the British area of operations.

That night I meet the First Cheshire's sergeants in their mess, a tough, cheerful and professional bunch; these are the people who really make this unit work. Afterwards we eat a British Army meal in a British Army tent with Colonel Bob's officers. This is a young officers' war and these young men, often in their early or mid twenties, are the convoy commanders who have to interpose themselves and their men between two warring sides intent on destroying each other and fully armed to do so. They have, often by the force of their personality alone, to convince both warring sides to think of the innocents caught in the middle. It is a task requiring coolness, fine judgement and extreme courage.

The next morning, after the usual British Army breakfast in which beans play a large and traditional part, I am off with Colonel Bob to the front line between the Muslims and the Serbs. Above us towers the Vlasic, a huge snow-covered mountain dominating both the British base and the whole of the Vitez area. With a pair of binoculars, it is possible to see the Serb heavy gun positions which have the British base well within their range, but have so far only been used to destroy the predominantly Muslim towns at their mercy in the valley below.

We travel in a small military convoy, made up of Colonal Bob's armoured car and a few others, through Travnik and on to the neighbouring small village of Turbe. Travnik shows all the signs of recent heavy shelling. The Serb gunners on the hill have been making a special attempt to knock down the mosque whose tall minaret has taken a direct hit.

In Turbe, we are about 150 yards from the front line. We stop in the little town square and go into the defending Muslim force's headquarters, accompanied by a few rounds of machine-gun fire from the Serbs on the hill above us. Inside it is dark, with only narrow shafts of sunlight coming through the slats of boarded windows. It takes my eyes a moment to adjust to the light. In the room is the local commander of the Bosnian Government Army and his officers, a big table, some maps, a pot of Turkish coffee, a bottle of slivovitz and a jumble of half-full ash trays, glasses and unwashed cups. The commander and his men look haggard and sunken eyed. Through an interpreter, a young British officer who studied Serbo-Croat at university, he tells us that they have had a hard night of it. The Serbs brought down tanks and despite some losses managed to drive the Bosnian front line back in two places. The commander points to the revolver on his belt. 'This is what I have,' he says. 'My Serb opposite number has a howitzer.' We can hear a distant crump of artillery shells and a short exchange of machine-gun fire outside.

After an hour, two cups of coffee, some slivovitz and a glass of reciprocal whisky brought by Colonel Bob, we leave – once again with a few shots over our heads as a parting gesture from the nearby Serb front line.

On the way back down the valley to Travnik a single mortar bomb lands ten yards from us with a sharp crack. I can smell the cordite as we drive through it and Colonel Bob swears loudly over the radio. I tense myself, expecting the follow up rounds, but they never come. Probably a Serb gunner on the hills who had this point well registered and is not prepared to waste ammunition.

Behind us, a following BBC crew manages to get a shot of the mortar bomb exploding, one amongst many hundreds which fall everyday in this war. The pictures run on all the news headlines for the rest of the day in Britain. One of the First Cheshire officers later comments 'In this war, it's not what happens, but what happens on film that counts.'

Afterwards we go to visit the local aid warehouse of the United Nations High Commission for Refugees (UNHCR). Here a young Briton is organising aid distribution and I meet other British civilians who are driving unarmed trucks throughout this area to get aid through to people of a country most of them will probably never even have heard of before. These are the real unsung heroes of this war – ordinary people from ordinary towns throughout Britain who want to do something to help and are prepared to risk their lives to do it. The tragedy in Bosnia is, it seems, the Spanish civil war of our generation – an event whose suffering and significance is understood more clearly by ordinary people than by many of our leaders and whose impact has stirred many of them to individual action to compensate for the failure of governments.

Then on over the mountains to Zenice, the beautiful Muslim town which lies in the centre of the British area. On the way we pass through alpine meadows and cows grazing on the high pastures and peaceful little villages whose peasant inhabitants must be as bewildered as they are terrified by the beast that has suddenly been unleashed amongst them, killing their uncompre-hending children and taking an ancient revenge on their simple houses and quiet communities.

In Zenice we visit the office of the International Committee of the Red Cross, run by a harassed young Swiss lady, whose doors are besieged by pleading faces desperate for news about their loved ones lost in villages swallowed up by the war or incarcerated in the dreadful Serb prison camps which I visited four months earlier.

Here we leave Colonel Bob and make our way down the valley to the UN forces forward headquarters at Kisseljac. Again, the senior officer who meets me is British, Brigadier Cordy Simpson. He is a cavalryman, whose spare frame, clipped vowels and efficient briefing takes me, despite the scene outside, straight back to Sandhurst. He has to go into Sarajevo almost every day in an unprotected Land Rover, because the British Government has said they cannot afford to give him a protected one. He tells me that the UN headquarters here is broke and cannot even pay their bills to the local Bosnian suppliers, because national governments have not paid their contributions to the UN operation – he tells me he has to spend much of his time ringing up governments begging them to pay their dues and has even had one respond with the well-known excuse, much used by small traders in difficulty: the cheque is in the post.

After a short break we head off for Sarajevo. This is my third visit to the city, but the sight of it still comes as a shock. We pass through the Serb check points which now have a stranglehold on the city and through the wrecked suburb of Otez, recently taken by Serb forces in hand-to-hand fighting at terrible cost. UN officials tell me that the shattered buildings still contain many dead bodies which have not yet been removed.

Sarajevo has taken a dreadful pounding since I left. There is scarcely a building left untouched or a pane of glass intact. Many of the suburbs where the fighting has been fiercest are little more than rubble, home now only for the rats and the snipers that plague the city.

We travel through the airport, which is currently closed because of shelling, and cross the fly-over along which, only a few years ago, the competitors and spectators for the Sarajevo Winter Olympics travelled. These days, this is not a place to loiter: it is a favourite spot for snipers. At the headquarters of the Sarajevo UN organisation in the old Post Telephone and Telecommunications building I meet Larry Hollingsworth again.

I first met Larry when I flew to Sarajevo with the RAF in August, two months after the siege had started. At that stage he was based at the airport and we shared a bunker together, as shells and mortars fell on the city around us. If there is a single person responsible for the fact that Sarajevo has survived a siege which has now gone on longer than Stalingrad, it is Larry Hollingsworth. He is an ex-British Army officer who joined the UNHCR. When aid first started reaching Sarajevo, it was Larry, together with two young British airforce officers who took over the storage and warehousing at Sarajevo airport, who organised the offloading of aircraft and began to put a distribution network together. Since then Larry, who has a rotund frame, a famous bushy white beard and a strong propensity for wearing ridiculous hats, has travelled, totally unarmed and in most cases unprotected, to every corner of the city and beyond. In, out and across front lines and often through the teeth of the fighting, he has gone wherever it was necessary to go in order to deliver his precious food, medicine and assistance. He seems fearless and completely impervious to intimidation. The UN is not universally popular in Sarajevo, but Larry is known and respected by every side.

Later in the afternoon, Larry takes me to the graveyard in Sarajevo. Here, at least, the dead lie in the same plot: there is no ethnic separation. Christian, Serb and Muslim lie side by side. But there are so many dead that they are running out of space in Sarajevo cemetery, so they are beginning to dig graves on the neighbouring football pitch – the snipers long ago put a stop to football matches. Around me most of the trees have been cut down for firewood. The depths of winter will soon be here and the ground will become frozen. So they have dug two or three hundred more graves, which ought to be sufficient for those who will be killed before the ground thaws in the spring again.

Afterwards I visit Sarajevo's two hospitals where Larry wants me to see the conditions. In the first hospital the doctors show me the shell holes in the wall of the intensive care unit where the Serbs shelled the hospital the day before. In a nearby bed a soldier is dying with a terrible throat wound and a young man has just returned from having his leg amputated. The doctor tells me he has no general anaesthetic, no plasma and no antibiotics.

In the second hospital they have re-positioned the 'intensive care unit' to the middle of the building in order to protect it from the shelling. It is no more than a small room crowded with haggard-looking nurses and doctors tending to patients on makeshift beds covered in sheets and blankets, many of which are stained with blood. In one bed, a doctor, who tells me she has been up for nearly thirty hours, shows me a young boy. He is about ten and his head, topped by a profusion of shining black hair, lies angelic on the pillow. He is not asleep, he is drugged and, she says, almost certainly dying. His stomach was ripped open by shrapnel from a mortar bomb earlier this morning. She, too, has no medical supplies. I stumble out, tears flowing as much with rage as pity. How is it that we cannot even supply these hospitals with the medicines they need?

Bristol, Hartcliffe and Withywood. 'Typical 1950s and 60s tower blocks, some scattered lower-rise housing and wide-open spaces.'

Planning for Real — 'not a mechanism for illustrating the architect's "solution", but a means for the community to express what it wants.'

Above: **Boundary Estate.**
'Oppressive outside, inside the
flats are damp, miserable and
overcrowded. Most have broken
windows and peeling walls.'

Left: **Adur.** 'The people really
seem keen to do their bit.'

Left: **Camden Training Centre.**
'Everyone has the potential to achieve if the training process is properly resourced.'
Below: 'What will I do after my year's training is over'?

Right: **Wapping Safeways.** 'Charles is for the first time in his life in a job and clearly proud of what he does.'

Below: **Bosnia.** 'All sit more or less patiently while young British soldiers try various methods to unblock the road.'

Nick South

Goodness knows what the nurses and doctors think of someone who cannot even control himself at the sight of a single tragedy, when they have to deal with so many, so constantly.

I then drive through the city to the UNHCR warehouses. Here, Captain Peter Jones, young Royal Corps of Transport officer, has been brought in to re-arrange the feeding of the city along more efficient lines. He tells me of his anxiety that we are still not getting sufficient food into the city. He is especially concerned because the warehouses are empty and there are no reserves if the winter weather clamps down, or the Serbs decide to close the aid corridors.

Throughout every Sarajevo day there is the almost continuous background crump and bang of shells falling randomly on the city. Apparently the Muslims made a successful attack somewhere last night and the Serb gunners have decided to take it out on Sarajevo's inhabitants. Of slightly more concern are the snipers, whose aim is more purposeful and whose daily 'score' is higher. We quite frequently hear the crack of a bullet passing by. These are known in Sarajevo as 'whizzers'.

That night Larry and I go up onto the roof of the UN headquarters and look down on Sarajevo. Here is a great European city, once famous as a centre of religious tolerance and multi-ethnic culture. There are still 380,000 people here. But tonight not a single light burns. All is darkness save for the tracer rounds and the occasional mortar and shell falling onto the buildings and streets around us.

The next day, Larry takes me across the front line to see the Serbs who have been shelling us. Here we have to pass along what Larry calls the 'Butmir 400', a stretch of 400 yards which runs between both front lines who often both decide that, since they have had a frustrating night and have not succeeded in killing each other, they might as well compensate by trying to kill passers by. But our journey is uneventful on this occasion. On the following day the fog is mercifully down and we are able to pass between the snipers, heard but unseen.

I leave Sarajevo in an armoured car driven by a Dane and containing, apart from me, some Canadian soldiers, a Belgian major and some Nepalese military police. The UN is a multi-national force in Bosnia. But I recall the words of my travelling companion, the military journalist, as we waited in the snow on the dirt track through the Dinaric Alps, two days ago. He said, 'You know, yours is the best little army in the world. You wait, wherever you see something good and effective happening in this chaotic war, you will find a Brit at the heart of it, making it happen.'

But it's more than that. Our soldiers and aid workers on the ground in Bosnia seem to have a better understanding of what can be done and what ought to be done than many of their political masters in London. The soldiers on the ground have worked out clear aims for what they do. But our politicians have not yet worked out the political objective that they are doing it for.

A young corporal in Vitez put it like this, 'We are allowed to keep people alive here by giving them food, but we are not allowed to stop them being killed by shells and bullets.' Back in the headquarters in Split the British senior commanders in the war realise that they are pioneers in a new kind of warfare in which British soldiers will be asked to risk their lives not just in defence of individual British interests, but also to uphold international law. One senior officer said to me, 'This is the way our soldiering will be in the future – our boss on the battlefield will increasingly be the UN and not the British Government. That means working out new techniques, new lines of command and a whole new attitude to the way we do our job. In Bosnia we are learning what to do as we go along. But what happens when the war is over? Will all the lessons be lost – and when the next war like this comes along, will we have to start from square one again? War is a serious business and unless both our Government and the UN realise that they must take this new kind of war seriously, then a lot of lives will be lost and a lot of operations like this one will end in tragedy and failure.'

Chapter 9

'I can give him a share in my colliery.'

18–20 January 1993

To Edinburgh to visit Monktonhall colliery, a mining co-operative set up by redundant miners. After visiting the mine offices, I stay the night with the mine chairman, Jackie Aitcheson, and his family. The following day Jackie takes me down with the morning shift, with whom I spend the day, coming above ground again at the end of the shift. Afterwards, home with Brian Davison, the chief electrical engineer, to spend the night with him and his family.

♦

The door clangs shut and the cage drops like a stone 3,000 feet to the shaft bottom.

My companions joke that they can tell by the way the cage drops who is on the winding gear and how many pints they had the night before. We descend to the bottom in ninety seconds.

I clutch the plastic box which Pat Aitcheson thrust into my hand as we left her house at 6.45a.m. on this raw Scottish January morning and try to look as though I am quite used to going to work like this. The box contains my 'slice' – two sandwiches, two bars of Kit Kat, a can of coke and an apple which are to be my lunch on the eight-hour shift we are about to start at Monktonhall, Britain's deepest pit and only operating mining co-operative.

My companions in the cage include Jackie Aitcheson and Angus Macdonald. Jackie, touslehaired, paunchy, with a wonderfully mobile face and a dry Scottish wit, is the chairman of Monktonhall miners' co-operative. He describes himself – accurately – as 'a bit of a romantic about coal'. He was born 'at the bottom of the bing [mining tip]', and left school at fifteen to go down the pit. He rose to become a union official, led the militant miners in the strike at the neighbouring Bilson Glen pit in 1985, was sacked, worked as a school janitor and was one of the three men who masterminded the setting up of Monktonhall co-operative.

Angus, whose job today is to look after me and make sure that I don't do anything stupid, has also been a miner all his life. He worked in British pits and in South Africa and Rhodesia. His sharp eyes, lined face and immediate air of authority instil a confidence and reassurance that I find comforting.

The previous day, in the bare managing offices Jackie and Angus had told me the story of Monktonhall. British mining as an organised industry probably began here 800 years ago, with the Cistercian monks exploiting the coal seams through which we are now dropping. Since then the livelihood of many generations of families in this area of Scotland has depended on coal.

In 1988, British Coal began closing these Scottish pits, starting with Bilson Glen. Local miners looked at the possibility of converting Bilson Glen into a co-operative, but the pit was closed before they got the chance to bid. But a group of Bilson Glen miners kept together and started to look for alternatives. Neighbouring Monktonhall, which had been mothballed by British Coal, was opened up and the co-operative launched in 1988. They started mining coal seriously in January 1993.

The battle to establish the co-operative was long and difficult. The powerful local Labour Party establishment and the council opposed them and the Coal Board did everything they could to stop them. Local Labour politicians saw the Monktonhall co-operative as a dangerous precedent, which would break their traditional grip on the mining working class. They were also convinced that they were going to win the 1992 election and had promised to re-open all the local pits. This would mean, they said, that *everyone* would go back to work, whereas the co-operative could only provide jobs for a few. Jackie and his wife Pat, until recently strong Labour Party supporters, both told me that they had never believed Labour would win the election. The Coal Board, like the local Labour Party, saw the Monktonhall Co-operative as a threat to their control of the mining industry.

In the end the miners realised that they would have to by-pass the local Labour Party which they had voted for all their lives and get directly involved in politics themselves. They contacted other politicians, including the local Conservatives in Edinburgh. A meeting was arranged in London with the minister responsible, David Heathcoat-Amory. He had promised to see them for half an hour. They had arrived ninety minutes late because of train delays, but apparently had so impressed the minister and his experts that the meeting had gone on for an hour and a half. In the end the minister promised moral support, but no money. Jackie says that the reason the Government helped was because it would embarrass Labour, not because their heart was in it. However, the Government's moral backing meant they were able to get the banks interested in investing.

The original plan was to use the colliery land as colateral. Each miner was to put in a stake of £2,000. But then, at the last moment, British Coal moved the goal posts, changing the terms from a straight buy-out to a lease. Jackie says that British Coal did all they could to make the launch of the co-operative as difficult as possible, stripping the place of all easily moveable machinery and even burning brand new mining clothing and oil skins, rather than leave them behind for the co-operative. In the end the co-operators were forced to raise the individual stake for each miner to £10,000.

Down the pit I asked my shift mates how they had found the money. A few had left safe, well-paid jobs in order to own their own job and return to the comradeship and challenge of coal mining again. But for most, the stake had been very difficult to find. Some had found the money from their redundancy payments. Some had mortgaged their houses, others had borrowed the money from family and friends. Many good miners had been turned away because they couldn't find the money. The banks had been useless. I was to hear of one young, would-be co-operative member who had gone to his bank manager to ask for help and had been told that a loan was no problem and the appropriate forms had been quickly produced and filled in. The last question on the form asked about the purpose of the loan. As soon as the bank manager heard that the £10,000 was to allow his client to own a stake in a coal mine, he tore up the form. A loan for a car, or a holiday, or a house extension was fine, the bank manager explained, but lending money to enable someone to get a job was out of the question.

The Monktonhall miners had no help in setting up the co-operative and had to decide on the structure for themselves. Practical assistance in forming co-operatives such as Monktonhall used to be provided by the Co-operative Development Agency, but the Government closed this down in 1990, saying that it was no longer needed. Each member of the co-operative holds an equal share and benefits from any dividend paid out. A board of directors is elected at the Annual General Meeting. The directors hold a monthly performance meeting and have the full rights of management, including discipline and sackings. But there is common status for all. Under British Coal, there had been forty-seven grades in the work force, with special car parks and canteens for managers. All this had gone. Jackie, like all his fellow directors, spends most of his day down the pit.

I had been somewhat taken aback by this, when, the day before I had been sitting in his office waiting to meet the chairman. A miner, grimy with coal dust and complete with helmet and safety equipment on his belt, wandered in, bade me a cheery hello and sat down at the chairman's desk. I asked where I might find Mr Aitcheson, the chairman. The reply was that I was looking at him!

In place of the forty-seven British Coal grades, the co-operative has three, which determine their level of pay. The weekly wage for all coal face workers, irrespective of their position, is £350; underground workers get £300 and surface workers £250.

Jackie had earlier explained, as we drove to the pit from his home through the cold black morning, that the coal at Monktonhall is some of the cleanest in Britain, having one of the lowest sulphur contents in Europe. British Coal had closed the pit because it was too expensive to mine. But the co-operative's overheads were so much lower that they were now able to mine at less than half British Coal's costs. 'Three hundred and fifty million years ago, mother nature put down this coal for us to work and get our living from,' Jackie explained to me. 'British Coal tried to stop us, but we've found a way to do it for ourselves. But now that we have picked the berries it is important to ensure that no one steals our jam. What I'm really worried about is that now we have made a success of it, someone else will move in and buy us out.'

Later, after getting kitted up with orange overalls, miner's helmet, knee pads, gloves, belt, boots, battery and emergency breathing apparatus, I met my shift mates, stamping their feet in the early morning cold and cracking jokes, mostly at my expense. We each collect a numbered brass tag off a board to enable quick calculation of who was down the pit in case of accidents and make our way to the rusty cage, dripping with water, which was now taking us all to our place of work.

At the shaft bottom we step out into a network of tunnels big enough to take a London tube train. These are well lit and ventilated. A low, clanking colliery train rolls past us, forcing us to take refuge in an alcove in the tunnel wall. We then make our way down one of the tunnels, our boots kicking up dust and my colleagues' raw jokes and laughter filling the air. After ten or fifteen minutes, we turn into a lower tunnel and start to walk, following the line of a conveyor belt down a steep incline towards the coal face.

At the end of this tunnel we come to a flat area, where there are some control panels. Here we leave our 'slice' boxes, to be returned to at lunch time, and go through an air lock and into a yet smaller tunnel, nine or ten feet high, leading to the coal face.

The roof and sides of this tunnel are supported by baulks of wood jammed into position between iron hoops which are called circle arch girders. By now the cold air of the surface has been replaced by a stiff, warm, humid breeze blowing up from the coal face itself. This ventilation, carefully engineered and constantly monitored, is essential to blow away the deadly methane which causes the fires and explosions that miners fear most. We are 3,800 feet below the surface and in total blackness except where our helmet lights shine.

The coal face itself lies at the end of this service tunnel and runs at right angels to it. At the far end of the face a similar but smaller service tunnel runs parallel to the one we are now in. The whole complex is like a U whose flattened bottom is the face. As the face advances, the roof is allowed to collapse behind it and the service tunnels are driven forward and propped (the technical term is 'brushed') to keep pace with the face.

Around me my shift mates seem instantly and silently to have transformed themselves from a group of friends rolling home after a men's night out at the pub, into a close-knit professional team, each competent at their own role and confident in the skills of their mates upon whom, for the next eight hours, their safety will depend. I have always been fascinated by the way human beings are willing to pit themselves against impossible forces by relying on teamwork and technology. Here, winning coal from a three-foot seam under three-quarters of a mile of rock, these men are doing this for a daily living.

The coal face itself is a scene of dust and noise and blackness and roaring machines and pools of light gathered around each miner's sweating body. You would not here, like Wilfred Owen, listen

> for a tale of leaves
> And smothered ferns
> Frond-forests, and the low sly lives
> Before the fauns.

This is an altogether more brutal and businesslike affair.

Angus takes me to the face. We enter, crawling, through a forest of hydraulic pit props in which my colleagues are already working, clearing rocks and building a stone wall to prop the roof where the face meets the service tunnel.

The next three hours are spent entirely on my hands and knees, glad of the knee pads, which bite painfully but are infinitely preferable to the sharp edges of the rocks over which we crawl. I soon have to put on the gloves too as my hands quickly become bruised and lacerated. At one stage a large rock falls without warning from the roof and rolls towards me. With no retreat, I put out my hand to try to stop it – a totally useless gesture, which only serves to give me a sharp bruise. Fortunately the rock runs out of momentum before reaching me, otherwise it would certainly have broken my leg.

Angus patiently explains that no miner would have been sitting where I was, since that was an obvious place of hazard for falling rocks. There seems to be a sixth sense about these people, who work and curse and joke in such a carefree manner, but always have some reserve, invisible force calculating where the danger is and minimising it for themselves and their fellows. All conversation is conducted by shouting at the threshold of your neighbour's ear, but it is the confined space which is most difficult to get used to.

The face tunnel, into which is fitted the cutting machine, a conveyor belt, and the miners who work them both, is about three feet high and ten feet wide.

The cutting machine itself is a huge affair that somehow reminds me of a prehistoric reptile whose flashing whirling teeth tear at the glistening narrow black seam which has been waiting for us down here for 350 million years. The cutter seems to fill the entire space, roaring up and down in a cloud of sparks and dust, cutting forward into the coal and pushing it onto the conveyor belt.

Perched on the back, Lexy Gay, the machine driver, curses and swears and gently controls the great beast so that it stays in the seam and does not cut into rock which would blunt the tynes (shearer picks) and have to be separated from the coal later. I notice that he positions the whirring disk of teeth about an inch below the top edge of the coal seam. The remaining uncut coal then drops off, leaving the rock ceiling grey, clean and smooth. Angus tells me that in his last mine a cutting machine driver went to the front of the machine to clear something from the cutting disk without immobilising the machine. The machine started, whirring the man's body on to the shearer picks and into the rock ceiling.

Running parallel with the cutting machine a conveyor belt carries the cut coal and rock down the face to the service tunnel and then, by a system of conveyors and lifts, to the surface for sorting. Behind this, in the remaining space left in the face tunnel, is the working area for the miners who, on all fours, tend the machines. This area, about three feet square, is protected by hydraulic ceiling supports. There are about 180 of these individual units positioned next to each other and forming a tunnel along the whole length of the face. Each unit is like a huge pair of jaws, big enough to take a squatting miner at work. The jaws are held open with vertical hydraulic rams pushing the top against the rock ceiling. And the whole unit is pushed up against the face by another set of hydraulic rams operating horizontally and pushing against the rock from the fallen roof of the previous face, whose ceiling has been allowed to collapse as the face moved forward.

As the new face is cut, the vertical rams are lowered and the horizontal rams push each unit forward to meet the rock face, together with the miner who is operating inside its open jaws. And always, when there is silence enough to hear it, there is the sound of the groaning and cracking of the roof above and of the rock falling over yesterday's cut, with sharp reverberating thuds which make the hydraulic units dance. Two months after my visit, Billy Gorman, a miner on this shift, was killed in a rock fall on this face.

I have a chat with Willy Martin, while following the cutting machine on its second cut. Willy is responsible for seeing that the high power electric cables feeding the cutter don't get snagged. He is a wiry diminutive Scot whose size seems designed for this kind of work. He tells me that he hopes that they will open another co-operative at the Francis pit in the Fife region. There the seam is eight to ten feet high. Willy will withdraw his stake from Monktonhall and re-invest it in 'The Francis' if they open it, as it's closer to his home. He is proud to be able to move his stake. He tells me that he is now employing the manager, rather than the manager employing him. But he is bitter about Michael Heseltine, who he says hasn't given them any help at all, and now seems certain to subsidise other British Coal pits in order to save his own political career, so undercutting the price of coal from Monktonhall.

Angus explains to me that this is a real fear. 'They haven't given us a penny. No one has ever rung us offering help or advice, or even assistance with overseas orders. They've just ignored us as soon as the political benefit of getting one over on the Labour Party ran out. We have opened up a pit that would have been lost. But they seem more interested in subsidising failed British Coal pits and undercutting our business.'

At around midday they blow a charge of dynamite in the neighbouring service tunnel. We all move down the face away from the blast and sit under a ceiling support with our backs to the explosion. In the confined space of the pit, all the sharp crack of an explosion that I am used to is lost. There is a dull reverberating thud which raises a lot of dust and loosens some roof rocks. For a few moments, the sharp, acrid smell of cordite fills the face area. Then we get back to our work.

Later Angus takes me crawling back the 150 yards or so to the main service tunnel from which we started. Here he shows me the 'stall'. This is a larger area at the end of the face where the cutting machines can turn at the end of their run. In days gone by it would have been where the pit ponies waited for their loads, hence the name. I remark to Angus at the cleanness of the break between the coal seam and the rock face above. He takes me into the stall and shows me the roof close up. He points to a concave indentation in the coal roof. 'This is the carbonised remains of an old tree stump,' he says and strikes the roof with his pick. A huge lump of coal falls out of the roof ('quite enough to kill a man' Angus tells me), leaving a neat hole and a clear view of the clean grey rock face above the seam.

I am then taken to do some 'brushing' on the roof of the service tunnel. Here I am introduced to Andy Bowds, 'Big Andy' because of his size. I help, in what I recognise to be a purely symbolic way, to shift a pile of fallen rock obstructing the access to the face. Andy does about four times the work that I do in the same space of time and doesn't end up panting and exhausted.

He tells me that his wife is expecting and should have had the baby by now. He makes some bluff rude comments about the fact that his wife is always late, but is clearly as proud and nervous about the birth as any expectant father 'I am hoping for a wee boy,' he says, 'then I can give him a share of my colliery.'

As we break for lunch I see one of my shift mates bend down and pick up a discarded bolt and put it carefully in his pocket. 'In the old days we used to leave them to get buried,' he tells me. 'But this is my pit now and this is my bolt and it costs, so I'm saving it.'

Lunch consisted of a half-hour break, taken back at the console area at about 2p.m. I am not a great lunch eater, but I was glad of the 'slice' Pat Aitcheson had put into my hand in what now seemed another world, eight hours previously. We return above ground at the end of the shift at 4p.m. The slope back up to the lift seems much steeper than on the way down.

Back on the surface there is tea to slake the dust and thirst and a shower to wash away most of the grime. I go home after work with Brian Davison and spend the evening with his delightful family. There is an excellent casserole and a bottle of good German wine and afterwards Brian and I go to the pub.

Brian, a quiet thoughtful man and a Geordie, also left school at fifteen and is now the colliery's chief electrical engineer. He went back early from the 1984 strike and told me that Arthur Scargill was the man chiefly responsible for the devastation of the coal industry. I ask him whether the fact that he was a 'blackleg' and Jackie Aitcheson was a famous militant strike leader creates tension. He tells me that in some communities the old bitterness still persists, but at Monktonhall they have decided that they are about building the future of coal and that means putting the past, however painful, behind them. The subject is never even discussed. As Jackie says, 'The water which has flowed under the bridge is gone and without our control – it's the water that's still to reach the bridge which we will build our future from.'

Brian tells me that he gave up a safe, well-paid job on the Channel Tunnel to invest in Monktonhall and be with his wife, Norma, and their two sons, Phil and Kris.

Earlier one of my shift mates described Brian as being like the pit canary – everyone trusted him and regarded him as a kind of weather vane for trouble. If Brian was happy with things, then they were probably all right. If he was worried that things were going wrong, then they probably were.

When I returned to the House of Commons the following day, despite the scrubbing, I still had the coal dust of Monktonhall face in my pores and under my finger nails.

———————

Chapter 10
'The bravest people in the world.'

25 January 1993

To Liverpool to visit the Eldonians, a housing and community co-operative in Vauxhall. Spent the day with the leading light of the Eldonians, Tony McCann. In the evening, attend a meeting of the Eldonian Development Trust and stay that night with Maureen McGuinness and her daughter Sharon, who live on the Eldonian estate.

◆

'The council and the politicians tried everything they could think of to stop us,' Tony McCann tells me. 'They bullied us, they threatened us, they tried to tempt us with offers of housing they thought we couldn't refuse. But we stuck together and in the end we won. Their biggest mistake was to think that, just because we come from one of the poorest areas of Liverpool, we were stupid. What they didn't bargain for was that we are just as clever as them. What they didn't realise was that they were dealing with the bravest people in the world.'

We are sitting in the Tony McCann Centre, the pleasant modern purpose-built office which contains the headquarters of the Eldonian community co-operative in the Vauxhall area of Liverpool. Tony has introduced me to some of his team who run the Eldonians: John Livingston, the local Labour councillor; Lizzy Jewkes, who is the administrator of the Eldonians' home for the frail and elderly; Mary Collins, who manages the home; Margaret Jackson, the manager of the Eldonian Development Trust; Ray Talbot, on secondment from United Biscuits to help her; and Paddy Bradley, who is the neighbourhood policeman and lives on the estate.

Outside the window, on one side, I can see dockside Liverpool in all its dereliction and decay: wind-blown wastelands, where factories used to stand; huddled rows of terraced houses shrinking under the brutal grey pillars of 1960s concrete deck-access flats; Victorian pubs, schools and churches, once proud and thriving along a busy road, now left crumbling, dingy and exposed after the tide of human activity had washed away from them.

But out of the other window, as if from a thousand miles away, a neat estate of bungalows and houses, double-glazed, different, modern, individual, yet somehow giving the impression of cohesion and common purpose. Tidy gardens, swept roads and all the signs of human care and pride which seems so absent in the decay which surrounds them.

This is the Eldonian Village and its father figure and prime moving force is Tony McCann. Tony is bluff, Liverpool Irish and looks it. He has sharp, alert eyes, the frame of a bull and the determination of an express train. They will tell you locally that without him there wouldn't be any Eldonians left in Liverpool. For the Eldonians take their name from Eldon Street, in an area Liverpool city council started to demolish twenty-five years ago and whose inhabitants they planned to scatter to the four corners of outer Liverpool. The war of independence between the Eldonians and Liverpool city council lasted a quarter of a century. It is the story of that war which Tony McCann is now telling me.

Vauxhall was the home of Liverpool's Irish community, who came to find work in the docks at the height of the 1840s potato famine. They were a close-knit community, but a very poor one. Cholera, ricketts, TB and other diseases which come with over-crowding and poverty were rife up to the 1920s and 30s. Infant mortality was high and education standards low. Maureen McGuinness, with whom I am to stay that night, was one of thirteen children, of whom only eight survived childhood. In the pre-war years the average life expectancy for children in this area was seven years.

Up to the early 1960s the Vauxhall community lived in tenements, or 'courts', each housing four or five families, and built around a courtyard, with a single outside lavatory and a single standpipe for water.

For most of this century, employment in this part of Liverpool depended on tobacco and sugar. The factories of Tate & Lyle and British American Tobacco dominated the area and its economy. In 1985, Tate & Lyle closed their gates and walked away from Vauxhall, leaving a derelict site and a destroyed economy as its legacy for one hundred years of loyal work from the Vauxhall community. They gave the factory site to the city – but it cost the city £2.1 million to clear the land.

BAT left shortly afterwards, leaving Liverpool with a vacant building, a derelict site and the vague prospect of a business park as a remembrance. And after that, the docks went. Unemployment in the area is now around 40 per cent, the highest in the city. The Vauxhall community had lost their jobs and their dignity almost over night. And Liverpool city council tried to make them lose their homes as well.

In 1963, under the city council slum clearance programme, the 'courts' were knocked down and replaced with some good standard deck-access flats, homes and maisonettes. Five years later, with scant warning, little explanation and no consultation, the city council decided to knock down some of these new flats to make way for the second Mersey Tunnel they had decided to build.

Eldon Street was not affected, but the residents were able to see what went on. The families were moved out and what was a close community was scattered to places such as Speke and Kirby, on the outskirts of Liverpool. Here there were neither new jobs nor old friends. Suicide and early death rates in the transplanted communities rose so alarmingly that the Home Office called in experts to advise what could be done to regenerate lost community spirit. A lot of money was spent – nothing was achieved.

Despite this the council decided in 1978 that the exercise was such a success that they would abolish all deck-access flats, which were regarded as being out of fashion. The city council called all tenants to a series of meetings. A week before they came to Eldon Street, 800 tenants from a neighbouring five-storey block of flats had been told by local councillors and officials that they had to leave in order to 'widen their horizons'. According to Tony McCann they meekly accepted their fate.

The Eldonians were next. But they were already planning their resistance. Five to six hundred of them gathered and told the council that they would not budge – that they were not going to let their community be broken up. Perplexed at this unexpected resistance, a local Labour councillor made a proposition: the Eldonians should conduct their own opinion survey of the estate. The council privately believed that the Eldonians couldn't conduct the kind of complex survey they demanded.

But, helped by the local priest of this strongly Catholic community, they completed the survey on time. It showed that 95 per cent were opposed to moving. The tenants explained that they knew that the flats were run down externally, but they had made them beautiful inside, so they weren't going to budge.

The council retaliated by threatening that if the Eldonians did not go, then they would all be put back five years on Liverpool's housing list. This, given the city's housing problem, was tantamount to saying that they would probably spend the rest of their days where they were. But the Eldonians stood firm. They decided that if the council would not house them without breaking up their community, then they had better build houses for themselves.

Fortunately the council, then under Labour control, changed political hands. Their local Labour councillor, the same one who had proposed the survey, was now supporting them. Working with the ruling Liberal group on the council, they started looking into the possibility of establishing a housing co-operative.

The Eldonians consulted some housing experts, who immediately wanted to take them over. But Tony McCann would have none of it. 'If you want to work with us, then you are going to have to realise that we are in charge, not you. We will interview you and if we don't want you then we won't have you. Your job is to help us get what we know we want, not to give us what you think is right.'

This has since become a cardinal Eldonian rule of the co-operative whenever experts are brought in. But they were, nevertheless, lucky in finding Jack McBane to steer the project. He understood both why they wanted to be in control and what they were trying to do. With his help five sites, one immediately ready for building, were found. The co-operative was established and all the Eldonians were called together. A hundred and twelve decided to join the co-operative, the rest decided to stay with the city council.

Then, in 1982, just as they were getting off the ground, the Toxteth riots exploded in the city. Central Government funds earmarked for the co-operative melted away into Toxteth projects.

Despite this set-back, the Eldonians kept going, meeting twice a week, exploring sites and interviewing community architects. They all had to learn how to read balance sheets, understand architects' plans, know how to lobby and persuade the city council. 'It was the best adult education you can give anyone,' Tony says, pointing out that not one of them had received anything more than the most basic education in schools regarded by most to be at the bottom of the Liverpool education system.

They decided that they would decapitate the top three floors of one block of flats and convert the remaining two floors into dedicated homes for the elderly, building bungalows alongside them so that the old and young from different generations could be kept together. When they started to plan the estate, they insisted on trying to re-create the atmosphere of the old courts, giving each house good views of their neighbour's so as to make it easier to watch over the next door property while the occupants are out. Paddy Bradley, the neighbourhood policeman, tells me estate crime rates are very low and that the closeness of the community and the layout of the houses makes this one of the easiest areas to police he has ever known.

In planning the estate, the Eldonians deliberately encouraged a wide variety of house designs. In the first fifty houses they built, there were twenty-seven different basic designs to choose from and any number of different building materials. The exterior design had to conform to one of the basic models, but inside the Eldonians could lay out their rooms exactly as they wished. Kitty McCann, an Eldonian to whom I later spoke said, 'We started off by just wanting a front door, but as soon as we got the hang of it there was no stopping us. I nearly drove my architect mad changing my mind about walls and chimney and where doors should be. But he was such a nice man and so patient – he even explained to me why some of the things I thought I wanted were wrong!'

Money was still a problem – but they were making real progress. Then in 1983 Derek Hatton and his militant Labour party took over Liverpool city council again. The Eldonians were told to stop everything dead in its tracks. Those who had already designed their own houses and made commitments were told that the building could go ahead, but the council would take over the houses and impose their own allocations once the houses were completed. The council's new masters justified this by saying that keeping the houses under council control was the only way to preserve jobs in the council's house maintenance department.

The Eldonians were also told that if they had any further ideas, they should go to the local Labour ward committee who would see that they were passed on to the city council for due consideration. But there was to be no more action at any level which was outside the city council control. Unfortunately, while many co-operative members had committed what was, for them, large sums of their personal money to their houses, they were still three weeks short of the purchase date for the land at the time the Labour militants took over.

Tony and the Eldonians tried to compromise. Would it be acceptable to the city council if the Eldonians used the council's maintenance department after they moved in and let the council nominate replacement tenants in the case of vacancies? The council refused. So the Eldonians had no alternative but to declare war.

They posed as magazine journalists to get access to their houses in order to photograph locks and take duplicates of the keys, so that Eldonians could move into their own houses just before the council's nominees arrived. They knew that the council would not dare to take court action because the council's legal case was questionable and they would not want the bad publicity. In one instance seven single people, who had each spent £700 in design and other commitments, managed to move in just half an hour before the council's tenants arrived.

However, they did not win every battle. Some houses were occupied by the council. The Eldonians took them to the high court with the help of a London barrister who gave his services at almost no cost. They won.

But they knew they couldn't stop there. Tony was determined to take the fight to the lion's den – he decided to recapture the local Labour party from the militants. He persuaded the local priest to withdraw permission for the militants to use a local church hall, knowing that the only other place for them to meet would be the local social club where Tony worked. Before the meeting started, he signed over 150 club members into the Labour party and then took the meeting over, kicked the militants out and took control of the local Ward Labour party. Violence was threatened, but when the militants saw the number of ex-dockers who had suddenly become members of their local Labour party, they decided that discretion was the better part of valour and beat a hasty retreat. Tony, who re-tells the story with obvious relish, says, 'We were determined to have a stake in our own lives and we weren't going to be stopped by anybody.'

But the council was not finished yet. In 1985, the Eldonians obtained £7 million on a loan from the Government. Using this as the downpayment, they worked out a cash flow based on the fact that most of the Eldonians would be in work. They decided that they could buy a site they had identified in the city. But then Tate & Lyle folded and everyone lost their jobs. They had to totally reconstruct the finances of the operation now that most people were on the dole.

In the end, they had to abandon the original site in favour of purchasing the old Tate & Lyle site on which they had all worked, which was going cheap. The council had wanted this site for building their own houses, but the Eldonians beat them to it. The council responded by refusing them planning permission on the grounds that the site was too smelly for human habitation as a result of the activities of the old sugar factory. 'Not too smelly for council tenants, but too smelly for Eldonians,' is Tony's comment.

The Eldonians, backed by the church and the local Catholic and Anglican bishops, appealed. Tony describes how, during the planning appeal, one of the council officials went on for an hour describing the problems of the site before, unable to contain himself any longer, the barrister representing the Eldonians pointed out to him that the map he was referring to was upside down!

Throughout this whole period the city council did everything they could to undermine the co-operative. They offered some co-operative members immediate housing in the best areas of Liverpool if they would leave the Eldonians. Those who refused found that requests for house repairs were delayed and the services they received from the council suddenly became minimal.

One Eldonian I spoke to had been moved out of her family house so that it could be knocked down to make way for a playground. Her family was told they would be moved to Kirby, on the outskirts of the city. They refused. The council told them that the only alternative accommodation they could find was in the notorious Sheehan Heights flats. It was the family's only way of staying in the community. So, with broken hearts, she and her family accepted. The council then put single drug addicts next door and refused to repair their flat when it developed a leak. There were constant break-ins despite heavily padlocked doors. She had stayed there for twenty years and had buried her mother, father and sister from the place. Finally she had been able to join the Eldonians and get a house with a little garden, which she had designed herself.

A few Eldonians were pressured into leaving. But most stayed. So, in the end, they won and went on to build their houses.

But not just their houses. They now have a residential care home for their elderly. This is no ordinary elderly home, for here people are not cared for by strangers and forced to spend their old age away from their friends. Here they remain within their community, grow old with their neighbours and are cared for by their own families. The home provides jobs for the community – for people like Mike, a trainee cook, whose mother works in the home and whose grandmother is a resident there.

And, sitting at the windows of the home, elderly residents will soon be able to watch their great grandchildren at play at the nursery they are building across the road. This too will provide jobs for the community and much-needed facilities for Liverpool. Littlewoods, one of the city's biggest employers, has already committed to taking 40 per cent of the new nursery's places for their workers and the Health and Safety Executive will take more. And, in September 1993, a village hall is due to open, providing space for general family use and creating more local jobs.

The Eldonians have insisted that the construction firm they have hired to build the new nursery uses as much local labour from the estate as possible, rather than bringing workers in from outside. They have worked with the contractor and the Construction Industry Training Board to design special training packages for their unemployed youngsters which lead to qualifications in building skills to help them get jobs in the future. A local garden centre has been established on the estate to provide more work.

They are now setting up a health forum to look at some of the endemic health problems of the area. Margaret Jackson, manager of the Eldonian Development Trust, says 'If you can design your own houses, why not your own health.' Plans for the future include a sports and recreation hall; development of a customised training initiative to help local people obtain job skills and the development of a youth enterprise centre to provide a focus for business and enterprise activity in the area.

To their great delight, the local newspaper had even, in a misprint, referred to them as the 'Old Etonians'!

But the Eldonians are not the only ones to benefit from their success. Their new estate and its facilities has completely changed the nature of the neighbourhood. Land values have gone up and the Eldonians have persuaded a major national construction firm to buy land and build a number of houses for sale, the first new private houses to be sold in the area in living memory. A supermarket has moved in to provide shopping facilities which had never been there before and small businesses are taking up residence under the nearby and previously derelict railway arches.

And now plans are well advanced for the construction of a neighbouring estate of 600 houses on the site of the old factories where this community used to earn their living. One hundred and fifty of these will be for the Eldonians and many are eagerly sought by those families who were dispersed by the council and now want to return home.

But, as I was later to hear at a meeting of the Eldonians Development Trust, in which local businessmen and women are involved and which is trying to get new employment into the area, there is now real worry that the Government's cut back in Urban Funding may well damage the future. The Trust has been going three years, and will have to survive on its own next year. Margaret Jackson compares this with the situation in America, where there are a greater variety of support mechanisms funded by both the public and the private sector to give backing to organisations like the Eldonians. I ask Tony who his greatest enemies have been in this remarkable story of determination, faith and renewal. He tells me, 'Politicians who think they know best and want all the power to themselves'.

Chapter 11

> **To the people of this community.**
> **This Post Office belongs to all of us. If we let it be robbed wear will our mothers and all old ones have to go – we have to stick together and protect Mr and Mrs Jones who keep it possible for the Post Office to be kept open for us all.**
>
> **PS Lets protect it like it was the other day.**

Sign, written in crayon,
above the counter of the sub-post office
in Upper Stanhope Street, Toxteth, Liverpool.

26 January 1993

Left the Eldonians and travelled across Liverpool city centre to Toxteth. Spend the day working in the post office with Doug and Rosemary Jones. Stay the night with them, before travelling back to London the following day.

◆

It is raining hard and the wet Liverpool pavements reflect back the dull grey sky and the drab buildings which frame it. It seems appropriate weather for such a place.

This is Granby Street, Toxteth, Liverpool 8. Maureen McGuinness had told me before I left the Eldonians in Vauxhall, no more than four miles away, that I mustn't go to Granby Street. Whites get killed there. James, who works in the Upper Stanhope Street post office, only 500 yards away, told me the same thing. It is nonsense, of course, like most of the myths about Toxteth.

The real tragedy of Toxteth is not just the unemployed, or the shattered buildings or even the drug culture. It is the indelible reputation stamped on this area of Liverpool by the riots in 1981. If even people in Liverpool see Toxteth as a no-go area, how can the rest of the country be convinced otherwise?

I have come here to work behind the counter with Doug Jones in the sub-post office in Stanhope Street. Doug, the postmaster, wiry, alert and in his late fifties, started life as an auctioneer. He then worked on the railways and in the voluntary sector. He used his spare time to study for university, and eventually qualified in social work and went on to take higher degrees in the social sciences. He spent a short time in the Cabinet Office working on policies for young people and then in senior positions in the social field. He eventually rose to become Director of Social Services for the Wirral. After a protracted dispute with Wirral council about the way things were done, Doug left and came to Toxteth, where, since 1983, he and his wife Rosemary have dedicated themselves to this tiny sub-post office in the very heart of one of Britain's most deprived and run-down inner-city areas. We are only a stone's throw from the site of the Toxteth riots which shook the nation in the summer of 1981.

His predecessor had been robbed and beaten up several times and had endured three gun attacks before being forced to leave. But Doug and Rosemary have used the post office as a centre for advice, welfare and social contact. He tells me that he always treats everyone who comes into his shop as clients – the Citizen's Charter is nothing new to him, he has always worked that way. He has been threatened several times, but paid no attention. In 1990, masked robbers burst into the post office with pick axes. People in the next door betting office heard what was happening, rushed in and chased the robbers away – hence the notice above the counter. Since then, any serious disturbance brings the customers from the betting office to his aid.

In this multi-ethnic community, where violence and lawlessness are common, Doug and Rosemary have become a loved and respected institution. When I asked one of their regulars why, the reply was because they treat Toxteth people like they would anyone else. This is not so elsewhere in Liverpool where the word Toxteth is regarded as a blight. Many shops in the city refuse credit and hire purchase to those who have an address in the area.

Drugs are rife here and the evidence of their use plentiful. There used to be some derelict houses opposite the post office shop which had been wrecked and set on fire during the riots. To Doug's horror, he had found young kids playing in them among the discarded syringes. He had to persuade the city council to demolish the houses in order to get rid of the menace.

It is Doug who has accompanied me to Granby Street, where in the rain, we are walking towards the Granby Street post office. It is 9.30a.m. and there are few people about. The street is said to be the home of most of the drug dealers in Liverpool, but there is no sign of them now. There are bright, multi-coloured shops selling groceries to the minority ethnic population in the area (mostly black) and there is a heavily barred and fortified off-licence, where we stop and have a chat to the owners.

Here and there are empty spaces left by houses burnt out during the riots. Every house seems to have at least one boarded-up window, staring sightlessly onto the rain-swept street. The few people around are huddling in doorways or, heads down against the rain, hurrying towards their individual destinations. This is neither the weather nor the area for casual street conversations.

They are building a new police post, or 'cop-shop', on the street. It has already been fire bombed once, but now they are using local labour to build it and there has been no further trouble.

The same cannot be said for the Granby Street sub-post office, which Doug and I call on to meet his colleague, Tony Murphy. Tony has been robbed countless times. On the last occasion the robbers had burrowed through from the next door house until only the thickness of the plaster on the wall separated them from the room where the safe is kept. When Tony opened the safe to start his morning's business, they burst through the covering plaster, beat him and robbed the safe.

Tony's nerves are gone. He has had enough and wants to leave. The Post Office authorities, who have been unable to find a replacement, wanted to close down Granby Street sub-post office. But local people, fearing the effect of a further withdrawal of services for the community in this already deprived area, persuaded the Post Office to think again. So Tony, by now a very worried and unhappy man, had to carry on.

As we leave Granby Street post office, I notice that the door is open on a run down Church Hall, opposite. Upstairs I find a group of people discussing a project to provide housing for offenders returning to the area. This is Adullam Homes, a Christian organisation which provides assistance to young people who are vulnerable, homeless or suffering from Aids, HIV or drug abuse. Here I find Godwin Bateren, better known in the area as Godwin the African. He is training some would-be Adullam workers. But he agrees to break from this and take me to see their project on Princes Avenue and afterwards to show me round Toxteth. Godwin is articulate, clever and committed to Toxteth. He is an ex-Merchant Navy Officer who lives in this part of Liverpool. He tells me that he has chosen to return home to manage the Adullam project because he hopes it will give him a chance to make a contribution to improving things in this area.

As we walk past small Victorian terraced houses and across the waste land to Princes Avenue, he reminds me that Toxteth contains the oldest black immigrant community in Europe. First established at the height of the slave trade in the late eighteenth century, it has none of the problems of newly arrived ethnic minorities who find it difficult to adjust and face hostility from the host community; Liverpool long ago accepted the black community in Toxteth. Toxteth's problem was not that it suffered hostility, but that it is ignored.

Time and again I hear from Toxteth residents of this resentment at being treated as the pariah area of Liverpool. Later on my visit, Doug Jones's daughter tells me of a new organisation being set up in the city to try to combat this. Called 'Common Purpose', it has been imported from the United States, where it has proved invaluable in breaking down barriers between the black ghettoes and the middle-class districts in American cities. Common Purpose runs educational programmes which bring together the young leaders and rising stars in all communities and ways of life right across the city. It enables them to learn and work together on projects and to get to know each other. In this way, personal friendships are established between people who later become the business and community leaders of their generation. These lines of communications have proved invaluable in times of crisis and in helping to generate a sense of common purpose for the whole of the city community.

Godwin and I soon arrive at Princes Avenue. Broad, tree shaded and lined with once noble Victorian houses, this was where the rich of Liverpool used to live. Today, Princes Avenue is where you drive through quickly to get past Toxteth and into the city. The houses which are empty are boarded up and those which are occupied are used as flats for a shifting population. Everywhere there is peeling paint, blackened windows and wilderness gardens.

It is one of these houses that Godwin is converting into units to provide a home for fourteen young local ex-offenders. He complains to me that he would have liked to see the construction work being used to give jobs and training to local unemployed, but instead the builders had been brought in from outside.

He takes me round, explaining that a lot of care has been taken to make each flat unit different and to give occupants both privacy and a sense of personal worth. Godwin says 'You have to remember that these youngsters have spent their whole life believing that they were of no importance to society – that the only way they were likely to get anything was to take it. I believe in firm punishment for criminals. But I also think we have to break the cycle of rejection and neglect, if we are to persuade young people who have known nothing but the bottom not to return to criminality.'

Afterwards I walk back to the Princes Road sub-post office, to meet Paul Hurst, the community policeman. Paul is white, in his forties and has worked in this area for four years. He loves it and tells me that he has been offered chances to move on, but has always rejected them. He has no further ambition but to play his part to help Toxteth and its people. But then Paul is rather an unusual policeman doing a rather unusual job.

He insists on walking the streets of Toxteth day and night alone because this is less threatening and enables him to communicate better with people in the community. In an area where the police are dangerously unpopular, he seems to be respected by all. Over his four years he has worked extensively in the local schools, where the children know him by his first name. Many are now adults and still refer to him as 'Paul', to the consternation and concern of the older inhabitants, who are more used to treating the police as the enemy. Paul considers this something of a breakthrough and tells me that he can now begin to see the first small effects of his style of policing bearing fruit in growing trust between himself and the community.

But Paul tells me that his bosses don't like policemen to stay on the same beat for too long. At headquarters, they spend their time moving people around so that they never really get to know their community. And they are more interested in league tables and charts on walls than on what makes for effective policing on the ground. In his previous job, Paul was told that his arrest rate hadn't been high enough. But in Paul's view, a policeman should be judged as much by how many crimes he prevents, as by how many arrests he makes.

Later Candy Smith, a friend of Doug's, comes into the post office and we chat about Toxteth. She was born and bred here. Like so many in this community, she cares for Toxteth and wants to do what she can to help. She tells me that there is real anger in the community about Somali refugees from the war zone being moved into the area and getting facilities which have been denied those who have lived here all their lives. She also expresses concern about the consequences of the Government care in the community programme, which has resulted in pathetic groups of mentally handicapped wandering the streets with nowhere to go. She has put several up herself, but the problem is too big for one individual to cope with.

Candy takes me to see the multi-cultural development network which is housed nearby. Here local colleges provide facilities to train local youngsters in child care, secretarial skills and catering. Its future is now threatened because of cut backs in funding. Afterwards I visit the local school and chat with the harassed headmaster who tells me that his biggest problem is lack of resources. They simply do not have sufficient teaching staff to give the children the kind of individual attention which they need if they are to have any chance of overcoming the disadvantages of their background and break free. Even the building is falling down; there is dry rot in the Victorian timbers, but the city council does not have the money to repair it. We visit the nursery, where, as in Peckham, I notice that, grindingly poor though this neighbourhood may be, every child is turned out impeccably for school.

In the evening I meet David Ogungburo, the author of the notice above the post office counter. David, self effacing, quietly spoken, with splendid dreadlocks, left school at fifteen. He is now forty. He says, 'Life is finished for me, but I am determined to do what I can to make this place better for the youngsters and the elders.' He has started reading again and is now studying for a social work qualification. Goodness knows what he might have achieved had he had received anything like a decent education.

David agrees to take me round Toxteth that night. We arrange to meet at 8.30p.m.

In the darkness, the place looks even more desolate and menacing. The open spaces are now empty, even of the casual passer by; I stumble a good deal on the pock-marked roads and broken pavements; most of the lights in the back alleys and smaller streets are out. I am glad to have David with me when, on several occasions, shapeless figures loom suddenly out of the darkness, and he is able to address them by their Christian names.

Twice we pass the entrance to a pub and I suggest we pop in. He replies 'no, too heavy'. But we find a place for a drink in the end. I ask David what he thinks needs to be done to give Toxteth new hope. 'The first thing,' he says 'is to give us a chance. Most people, even in Liverpool, think Toxteth is a no-go area – a dead loss. That's not right. When you look back in time at how things were in Liverpool 8 in the 1950s, most of the people of this community owned their own homes, including my father.

'The community spirits were very high, even though there was a lot of poverty and hard times; people had their own independence. The Liverpool docks were always busy and there was always something interesting. However then the Liverpool city council took our homes, took our independence away and made us dependent on them.

'Now, in the 1990s you can see the outcome in the despair of the people who live here and the conditions of the houses they live in. It is almost impossible to get repairs done – and privatisation has made it even harder. The sixties and seventies were the turning point in Liverpool. The bobby on the beat that you could talk to as a child and who everybody liked had gone and was replaced by those who everybody disliked. But there is still tremendous community spirit here and there are lots of people like me who are prepared to make things better if only we can get the chance. The second thing is to make us feel we own what is going on – that we are in charge. We have had too many experts come into Toxteth telling us what to do. They build us things without asking whether it is what we want. And then, even when there is such high unemployment in this area, they bring in people from outside to do the jobs. I tell you man, they are lost from the start. This may look a rotten place to you, but underneath this is a proud place, with proud people, lots of whom don't want this to be a centre for drugs and such and would do a lot to clean it up, if only they got a chance.'

As I leave Liverpool the following morning it is difficult not to reflect on the similarity between David Ogungburo's words and those of Tony McCann and the contrast between the Eldonians' success in Vauxhall and the desolation of Toxteth.

Chapter 12

'We tend to see crime as a problem for the police – unless we realise crime is a problem for all of us we will never beat it.'

1 February 1993

To Solihull to spend a day with Ollie Goode and the Solihull Crime Reduction Programme (SCRP). Spend the night with Ollie and his family.

◆

The woman is shaking and white with shock, even though it is twenty minutes or so since she had called the police. We had driven at high speed through the Solihull rush hour to the neat, well-kept suburban road in which she and her husband live. It is our third call in the brief hour I have been with this evening patrol of the West Midland Police. We have already visited a house on a council estate where a child's bicycle had been stolen and the home of a young British Airways stewardess, who returned home from Birmingham International Airport to find that her house had been broken into. The burglar failed to force the catches on her window and had to break the glass, alerting the next-door neighbour, who called the police.

Our present victim is not so lucky. She and her husband have lost some French francs left over from a recent skiing holiday and some jewellery. Still, it could have been worse. Once again, the burglar had been disturbed, this time by the wife returning home. By the broken back window are piled a collection of speakers and hi-fi equipment ready to be carried out of the house.

'Probably the same team who were disturbed at our previous call,' the young policeman says to his colleague. Then, turning to the victims, he adds, 'At this time of the year thieves wait outside around the time people return from work. If no lights go on in the house they know that there is no one at home and in they go. The cheapest, most effective thing people in estates like this can buy is a time switch to put the lights on in the evening when you are not at home.'

I watch as the two policemen go about their business with quiet professionalism, reassuring the victims, taking notes of the lost items and quickly assessing what follow-up action can be taken. Afterwards, over a cup of tea, we talk with the victims. 'I feel I have had my body invaded,' the woman says. 'To think that they have been in my bedroom – everything will feel dirty now. The jewellery was nothing much – its the fact that they have been in my house and touched my things that frightens me. I shall never feel safe here again.'

As they leave the two policemen arrange for the crime prevention section to call round the next day. 'Home Office studies show that a house that has been burgled once is three or four times more likely to be done again,' one says. 'About 30 per cent of crime in this area is "second helping" thefts. Once thieves have found the way into a house they often return to have a second go a couple of weeks later. Changing and reinforcing the locks on properties which have already been burgled is a cheap and effective way of cutting back crime.'

Afterwards, in the car, my two police partners tell me that these are minor incidents on a quiet night. But the reaction of the victims is typical. We measure crime, one explains to me, by what the victim has lost. But this takes no account of the hidden damage done to the victims through shock, fear and loss of self-confidence – even from relatively minor crimes. 'We often forget the human aspects of crime which are hidden by the figures,' he says.

I have come to Solihull to learn about the Solihull Crime Reduction Programme, a cross community initiative to fight crime in this area of the West Midlands. Solihull is a relatively prosperous residential area which contains not only Birmingham international airport, but also the intersection of three of the country's busiest motorways. It was beginning to suffer badly from criminals attracted to the airport for rich pickings and the motorways which provide the mobility they need to get in and out of the area quickly.

In 1990, the local council got together with local business and the police to form a joint front against crime. What they formed was the Solihull Crime Reduction Programme. What they discovered was a new way to fight crime.

Earlier in the day, John Scampion, the chief executive of Solihull council, explained to me how, five years ago, they had called a meeting with the police, the probation service and voluntary agencies to discuss ways of reducing crime. They established two aims – crime prevention and raising awareness of crime in the area. But the initiative soon dissolved into a talking shop. So the council approached Crime Concern, the national crime prevention organisation which is jointly sponsored by the Home Office and private business.

Crime Concern agreed to back the scheme provided two conditions were fulfilled. Firstly, there would have to be a proper system of evaluation so that the effectiveness of the scheme could be measured against the money being put into it. And secondly, the programme would have to be set up as a separate, freestanding organisation. The council and other organisations could contribute funds, but, Crime Concern insisted, Solihull's Crime Reduction Programme had to be independent in its own right. This has turned out to be a crucial ingredient in their success, since the programme is able to act as honest broker between those who suffer from crime and those whose job it is to prevent it. It has also enabled the programme to act as a bridge between the authorities, who set the strategies and 'the grass roots' who have to come up with the ideas and initiatives. John Scampion explains, 'If initiatives are to work, they have to come from the bottom up. Unless people feel ownership of what they do, they won't believe in it and it won't work.' This is a principle I hear repeated time and again throughout the day.

Initially the police were very suspicious of Crime Concern's involvement, believing that the programme would intrude into their area of responsibility and that the multi-agency, partnership approach would restrict their freedom of action. But this was soon overcome, largely because of the personal commitment of Roy Mellor, Solihull police division's chief superintendent, and his advisor Peter Oakley. Roy later told me that he had been involved in crime prevention initiatives in other areas, but the Solihull Programme was by far the best he had experienced, precisely because the police had been prepared to relinquish a bit of control in return for a genuine partnership which pulled in the active commitment of people and bodies whose help the police would otherwise never have been able to get.

When Crime Concern joined the programme they agreed, jointly with the council, to support and help with the appointment of a project co-ordinator. Here they were lucky – they found Ollie Goode. Ollie, who has become the prime mover of the project, is a most unusual man. He spent six years as an army officer in the Worcesters and Foresters but left to become a probation officer shortly after getting married because he believed that the unsettled life of the army was bad for his children. But he found probation work too bureaucratic and felt that he was only dealing with the symptoms of crime not its causes. So, when the chance to work with the Solihull project came he took it.

Ollie Goode and the Solihull programme's steering group quickly realised that if they were to fight crime effectively everyone had to be involved: schools, the welfare organisations, business, voluntary bodies – the whole community. 'We tend to see crime as a problem for the police – unless we realise crime is a problem for us all we will never beat it,' Ollie says. 'The great mistake in fighting crime is to believe that there is a simple and easy solution. In fact the origins of crime are complex and go right to the heart of society – not just for the criminal, but for the victim, too. We have to start thinking long term, rather than short term – we have to change attitudes and that means supporting families and helping schools become more effective. We have to change the way we think, designing crime out of our buildings, making people aware that the way they behave can make them more likely to be victims. We have to re-construct a sense of trust between citizens and the authorities – especially the police. This alone can take years of patient work. People, and especially politicians, have to realise that fighting crime is not a single battle which can be won, it's a campaign that has to go on continuously.'

The Solihull programme has four aims. Firstly, to assist people to live in greater security; secondly, to build crime prevention measures into the activities of local business and statutory organisations; thirdly, to assist local people to develop techniques for tackling crime and the social problems which contribute to it; and fourthly to reduce those aspects of crime which cause most problems to people in the Solihull area.

Funding for the initial four years of the project came from the council (£80,000) and private industry (£150,000). To this, the Home Office has added a further £150,000 for action on drug abuse and the Department for Education has provided a further £100,000 for school-based projects related to crime prevention.

John Scampion said 'This is a lot of money – half a million pounds or so. But its not that much when you think of the cost of the average crime and include in it the cost of the justice system, insurance and the impact on personal health and productivity. We are very pleased. The council provided the initial funding, but that has now been multiplied eight times over from other source in cash and kind.'

Ollie Goode makes a different point. 'The real multiplier is not in money, but in resources,' he says 'With that money we have unlocked human resources worth many times more from individual and voluntary activity and community commitment from businesses, local parish councils, schools, all of which have now been mobilised in the battle against crime.'

Ollie started his work for the programme with a full crime survey of the whole area. This put him in touch with a wide range of local organisations whose work was affected by crime. It quickly became apparent that the programme would only succeed if they targeted their resources at those areas which were most affected by crime and which yielded the most cost-effective returns. Ollie identified five key areas to work in. Young people, both as victims and perpetrators of crime; old people, whose lives were being blighted by the fear of crime; crime against women; neighbourhood initiatives and management of town centres.

Martin Poole, a communications specialist seconded by Powergen to work with the Solihull programme, began to map out and categorise crime incidents. He constructed a demographic profile for each council ward, showing the levels of unemployment. He then produced crime profiles, marking and categorising each crime and where it occurred. This immediately showed up the pattern of crime in Solihull and where the team should apply their resources first.

One unexpected outcome showed the prevalence of bicycle theft. This had been regarded as a rather minor offence, but it was soon realised that bicycle theft is a big problem, not a small one. Aggregated nationally, bicycle theft accounts for millions of pounds worth of crime every year. In some areas teams of professional thieves will move in with a container, which they fill with sixty to seventy stolen bicycles in a few hours. In Solihull alone, the value of bicycle thefts is estimated to be well over £150,000 in a year.

The Solihull programme approached Eagle Star Insurance, who readily joined in. A team was formed, supported by the police, road safety, probation and social services to produce a detailed local survey. This threw up two clear patterns; in one area the survey showed a concentration of bicycle theft around complexes of shops. In another, most bicycle thefts were from private property, especially garages and sheds. In most cases crimes involved children and young people both as victims and perpetrators. The team then moved into the shopping areas, encouraging the use of bicycle racks and persuading shopkeepers to put up notices about bicycle security. They also initiated a competition at local schools for new ideas to tackle bicycle crime and raise students' awareness of security. Already some very useful suggestions have come from the school children that will be passed on to council planners and can be used in local and national publicity.

Meanwhile, Ollie initiated a survey designed to discover what most concerns young people in the area. He chose a single whole year group of fourteen and fifteen year olds in a local school. This study threw up startling results about the extent to which young people are affected by and involved in crime. In the sample he chose, two out of three youngsters had taken something from someone else, two out of five had damaged property, one in five had used or possessed substances such as solvents, one in ten had used illegal substances, seven in ten had consumed alcohol without their parent's knowledge and one in three had been involved in violence against other people. But the survey also showed the extent to which young people are the victims of crime as well. Two out of five had been harassed or threatened, one in four had property damaged at school, two in three had property stolen at school and 100 per cent of those surveyed said they would be prepared to help friends whom they felt were in trouble.

One of the most worrying aspects revealed in the survey was the extent to which young people did not go to their parents or the authorities for advice. Eighty-eight per cent of the young people surveyed preferred to go to a friend for help; 50 per cent would go to a youth worker; 40 per cent to their doctor, 12 per cent to their teacher, but only 1 per cent would go to their parents and almost none to the police.

The survey also identified a number of key concerns amongst young teenagers. Top of these came fear of bullying, followed by substance abuse, followed by concern about personal safety and then worry about being the victim of theft. Ollie decided that if he was to tackle crime at large, he had better start at the beginning; at school. He explained to me that success depended on tackling the concerns as the youngsters saw them and asking them to propose initiatives.

A number of projects were launched in local schools as a result of this approach. At Light Hall school, a large and progressive Solihull comprehensive, I saw a play about bullying, written and produced by the students with the assistance of a professional theatre company which specialises in this kind of school-based work. I was sceptical at first, but, chatting to the pupils afterwards, there was no doubt that it had an effect on them. Ollie is convinced that bullying is the way many young people become involved in a pattern of violence which continues later and that much of it is cross generational and starts in the home. Input by young people had helped the school to develop its own policy on bullying.

A second play, originally written by eight to ten year olds in Manchester, illustrated the dangers of car theft. It was designed to help the participants build up assertiveness and resist peer pressure which is so often a feature of car theft and joy riding. Working with the probation service, police, social workers and schools, the Solihull programme had used the play as part of a half-day workshop for over 600 pupils in five local schools. The early results of this work are, Ollie says, very encouraging and demonstrate how effective imaginative work of this kind can be.

Afterwards I was taken to see a number of other initiatives launched in partnership between the Solihull programme, the local police and organisations, including one progressive parish council. These included a scheme, co-ordinated by the police and the parish council, to provide activities for local school children during the summer holidays. The aim was not just to occupy youngsters, but also to provide a medium in which young people could meet local police officers out of uniform and in an informal setting. One policeman told me that this was already transforming the relationship between police and youngsters in the area. Originally funded by TSB, the project has been so successful that it is now funded entirely by local businesses.

In order to tackle the youngsters' concerns about personal safety, the programme has also brought together representatives of the police, a firm of builders, the gas board, British Telecom, the water board and the other utilities and got them to sponsor and organise a day event in which ten to eleven-year-olds from local schools participate in an activities-based competition designed to illustrate the potential hazards they could confront in modern society. Each participating organisation set up a potentially dangerous situation and challenged the school children to identify the hazards and play act safe reactions to them. A prize of £200 worth of books was donated by Rover for the best team. One thousand one hundred children took part in these safety days last year. 'Better than Alton Towers,' was the verdict of one of the youngsters who did it. 'Better than a fortnight in the classroom,' was the verdict of one of the teachers. 'We are becoming a victim of our own success,' was the complaint of the organisers, 'now everyone wants to do it – but I don't know where we will get the money from next year.' One told me, 'This sort of event changes the way safety issues are tackled in the classroom and replaces fear with confidence in children.'

Another programme was being developed to counter drug and substance abuse. Once again, this was organised on a peer group basis, using the youngsters themselves to tackle the problem. Since Ollie's original survey showed that most young people will confide in a friend about their problems, the organisers decided to get together a group of volunteers aged between sixteen and twenty-one and train them up as 'peer educators' and advisers on drugs. One of the drug scheme workers tells me, 'We provide the framework in which the youngsters do the learning. We work with them and do not attempt to moralise about what they do. We provide training in the effect of drugs and then provide them with communications skills, information on substances, advice on where to get help, training on how to resist peer pressure and the skills to say no to 'persuaders'. Then the young people themselves become outreach workers in their own peer group. And they are much more effective than any adult can be. Our aim is not so much to solve the drugs problem we have, but to strengthen the community's defences against further drugs coming in.' To test the validity of the scheme, the programme had set up parallel pilot schemes; one in a local school; one in a youth group and one in a sixth form college. They had advertised in the local papers and a flood of volunteers had come forward – mostly from youngsters who were concerned about drugs or had friends who had been involved, bearing out the results of Ollie's survey that youngsters wanted to help their friends in trouble if given the chance to do so.

In one Solihull estate another project is working with young people at risk of offending by seeking to bridge the gap between local adults and young people. Helena, a lively youth worker from Dudley who has come to work on the project, explains how many instances of minor crime stem from a lack of organised activity, particularly during weekends and holidays. The Kickstart project brings young and old together to plan and organise local activities, make better use of facilities already in the area and help to realise young people's own ideas. The project is aimed at reducing minor crime, increasing the confidence of local people in their own abilities and lessening the fears that some people have of young people.

Helena describes how, in one area, older people were constantly complaining during holiday periods about disturbances from youngsters and asking the police to 'move them on'. Helena brought the two groups together and got them to describe the problem as they saw it. To the elderly, the problem was noise and disturbances. To the young, it was having nowhere to go and nothing to do. The two groups got together to lobby the council to provide leisure facilities locally. 'I don't know if they will succeed, but at the end of the process they understand each other better and are more likely to work together, rather than fighting each other in the future.'

Later, over dinner with Ollie and his family, I ask him to measure the success of the scheme to date. 'It's early days at the moment,' he replies. 'The scheme has really only just started and it will take a little more time before we are sure of our results. However, the first indications are promising. The national increase in crime last year was 14 per cent. In the West Midlands, the average was 9 per cent. But here in Solihull, we had an increase of only 2 per cent. There has been a particularly interesting reduction in car-related crime, which makes up about 40 per cent of all crime and in which the juvenile involvement is very high. But I do not want to put any weight on these figures, since they are for one year only. Our success here cannot yet be measured in figures. But what I am confident we have done is begin the process of mobilising the whole community in the battle against crime. My real worry is where the money will come from to continue the work on a permanent basis. The Government seems to think that if we start this and it is successful, then funds will come from private and business sources. I doubt it in the long term. This project got off the ground in the first place because the local council was prepared to "pump prime" it with funds and then draw others in. It will almost certainly need core funding from the public sector if it is to survive. I think, in Solihull, we are beginning to work out an effective framework for a serious approach to tackling crime. The real question for the politicians is whether they are serious about a long-term approach to fighting crime, or just want a few quick fixes for political purposes.'

Chapter 13

'How shall I bring up my kids in this?'

4 February 1993

I wanted to return to Peckham for a second visit. I arranged to spend the day with Judy, an outreach worker at the Peckham First Stop Crime Shop. In the evening, out with the local police in their fast response car. That night, stay with Judy and her husband Don.

◆

'I have lived here five years and been mugged five times and sexually assaulted twice,' the woman says.

The fog rolls in billows past her down the long alleyway onto which flats open like prison cells. It muffles shapes and coalesces into a single dark menace a group of youths, mostly white, who are hanging around a recess in the walkway. The sodium lights struggle against the gloom, throwing yellow circles where they succeed and casting even deeper pits of black shadow at every corner, behind every wall and down every stairwell where they cannot reach.

Under the flats, garages, dark even during the day, and full of litter including syringes and discarded crack pipes, provide convenient refuges for muggers, drug addicts and the dealers who feed the craze which drives the crime that terrifies this neighbourhood. This is a landscape designed for predator and prey. Those who pass through it do so hurriedly and, as far as possible, not alone. I am not alone, but still the hairs on the back of my neck prickle.

These are the North Camden, North Peckham and Gloucester Grove estates in London – a 1960s-built maze of deck access council flats and tower blocks which are home to around 16,000 people in South London. I am here with Judy, a bright young West Indian who works in the recently opened 'First Stop Crime Shop' on the estate, Saleem, chairman of the North Peckham estate tenants' association and Brad Smith, out of uniform, the neighbourhood policeman.

The woman Judy and I are speaking to is terrified to be stopped and clearly anxious to get back behind the safety of her locked and barred front door. Every flat here is a fortress against the jungle outside and, after dark, a prison for its occupants. But even that protection is not always enough. We have just visited sixty-five-year-old Mr McCourt in his downstairs flat. Burglars with knives have raided his home five times in as many years and robbed him in the street twice.

That morning I had called on the Fernandes family, who have six children and have already been burgled, even though they have only been here six months. Mrs Fernandes and her husband have beautifully decorated their flat inside, but lock and bar their front door after dark and would never let their children outside after six in the evening, even in the summer. 'In the evening, we close the door and try to forget about what's outside,' she says.

A neighbour, Mr Ryan, is sixty-three, asthmatic and has a weak heart. But that didn't stop young white robbers from trapping him on his way home, beating him up, stealing £45 and leaving him bruised, with a broken rib and severely cut face. Even he was luckier than an eighty-six-year-old woman neighbour who was recently beaten, robbed, stripped and raped in her own flat.

This is an estate that might have been designed for crime. Every corner is blind, every stairwell dark and foreboding, every recess a trap. The squares between the blocks of flats, no doubt originally intended as tasteful estate gardens, have become quagmires of mud, trees, bushes and blackness. Most of the greenery has disappeared and been replaced by cars, both the quick and the dead, parked in jumbled disorder where their owners last left them. And everywhere the walkways run in a three-dimensional maze of escape routes through corridors and tunnels and stairs.

In nearby Gloucester Grove, the five-storey blocks are each connected by a tower containing the lift, the stairs and three bridges running in different directions on each floor. A recent knife gang was able to wait in the safety and comfort of the top floor, picking out their quarry as they crossed the wasteland below and then pouncing as the lift delivered their victim effort-lessly into their hands. Afterwards they had a choice of five directions in which to escape. In order to catch them the police had to mount a six-month observation culminating in an oper-ation which required thirty officers just to block off the escape routes.

In the 1960s, when the estate was being planned, an architect, well known for his work in American inner cities, warned the council that the design would prove a disaster to live in and a gift for criminals. He was thanked for his advice and ignored. Several years after the estate was built, the architect who designed it paid a visit and was horrified at what she saw. Shortly afterwards she is said to have committed suicide. Suicide rates for those who live on the estate are very high, too.

And the local council hasn't helped much either. They painted out the graffiti which covers the Gloucester Grove estate stair wells, ignoring warnings from the fire brigade about fire resistant paint. Someone set fire to a pile of refuse at the bottom of one of the stair well towers, turning the inside into a raging chim-ney of burning paint. An unwary resident, opening a passage door to get to the lift, was met by the fire ball which pursued him, forcing him to flee down the corridor and out of the window to his death.

And they have put here, among a bewildered and increasingly elderly group of whites and West Indians who have lived on the estate all their lives, Nigerians, Somalis, Vietnamese, each resentful of the most recent arrivals, each mutually suspicious, each living in an ethnic island of their own. Unemployment on the estate is 67 per cent and 35 per cent of the residents are old age pensioners, most of them white.

Selim says that when people leave here they do not take their cookers and fridges. The whole estate is so infested with cock-roaches that cookers and fridges, in which they live, have to be left behind or disposed of.

And to add a little extra misery to the physical desolation, the authorities have also put here the mentally handicapped, emp-tied from institutions under 'care in the community'. Pauline, a mental health worker, whom we had previously called on, told me that there are no resources to support them, so they are left to wander the corridors and alleyways like lost souls in hell.

Judy says the council has been swamped by problems and hasn't the resources to cope. The recent cut in the Government's Urban Programme have forced the council to shut down local initiatives to help the unemployed. Two local youth clubs have had their hours reduced and work with teenagers and drug users has been curtailed.

We later visit a sheltered housing unit where they tell us that things on the estate used to be very different. When it was first built it was regarded as being one of the most desirable council estates in London. The original community had been white and West Indian. But then other groups were moved in. Later on drugs got a hold and the whole place started to slide down hill and no one has been able to stop it.

One of the police officers in Peckham police station put the same point to me in a different way. He said that all the big chain stores were moving out of the area. 'C&A have gone; Sainsbury's are going; Marks and Spencers left two months ago. Once Marks goes, you're dead.'

Selim explains that the local politicians hadn't helped. They had two good councillors now, one black and one white, both living on the estate. But the Greater London Council had been a disaster. 'They told us we were deprived and they would give us things, when what we wanted was the chance to do things ourselves. They gave us a begging bowl, when what we wanted was a future. And they made our people freaks. We didn't know which 'minority' we were supposed to belong to, black, homosexual, female, straight or gay. Most people on the estate don't vote – they just don't trust politicians any longer.

'One of our problems,' Selim continues 'is that all the social workers and priests and experts who come and tell us what to do and how to live our lives are only here from 9 to 5. None of them actually live on the estate – they all live somewhere else.'

But things are, at last, beginning to change. The First Stop Crime Shop, jointly funded by the Government, the local council and the police, is spearheading the fight back against crime. The Shop, painted bright red and standing out in sharp contrast to the shuttered shops and broken windows on the Plaza in the

Camden estate, was set up as a half-way house between the residents and the police.It offers advice and help with crime prevention, victim support, personal safety and domestic violence. Judy, committed to making things better here, is one of four workers in the shop.

During my visit, one of the other workers, Ken, a lock fitter, was giving advice on the fitting of free locks to some residents who had just moved in, while Judy was dealing with Vicky who has come to see her to complain about the police not following up on a horrific assault she had recently suffered. Vicky agreed to tell me her story.

She is in her thirties, dressed in bright West Indian clothes, articulate and dignified. She tells me in a calm voice how she was approached by a drunken man, who she thought was of Nigerian origin, as she returned home to her flat on the nearby Aylesbury estate after doing her shopping about six weeks ago. She had not been able to get rid of the man by the time she had reached her block. She did not want to go straight home, because her children were there and she did not want him breaking in and harming them. So, as she reached the stairwell leading to her block, she turned to reason with him. He grabbed her and, holding a broken bottle against her face, he forced her into a conveniently unlocked boiler room on the ground floor. There he attacked her with the bottle, cutting her face, stomach, breasts and genitals. He attempted to rape her, but without success. Eventually her screams alerted a neighbour whose intervention, she believed, saved her life.

The police arrived quickly and were excellent in the immediate aftermath of the incident. When they went into the boiler room to inspect the scene of the assault, they found a dead body in a cupboard, which Vicky had not seen. But then the police investigation ran out of steam. No interview had been conducted with the neighbours and no forensic examinations were done on Vicky's clothes. Vicky explains to me that she has come to the First Stop Crime Shop because she can talk to Judy, but did not feel able to approach the police directly.

Judy tells me that she will take the matter up with the police at a liaison meeting the next day. She says that she has very good relations with the police in the Borough of Southwark, who go out of their way to support the First Stop Crime Shop and are doing their best to rebuild trust in the community.

And slowly, very slowly, self-confidence and a desire to do something to clean up the estate is coming back into this community. The council and the police have worked together to establish safe routes through the walkways, closing the worst of them off. Mending broken street and walkway lights is now treated as a priority. The underground garages are being progressively closed and shuttered off.

This more optimistic view is re-enforced by Dennis, a young West Indian whom I meet later, playing dominos with his friends. He recently prevented an assault on a local doctor and made a citizen's arrest of the assailant; unheard of in most communities, dangerous in this one. Dennis tells me that he and his friends have decided that they have had enough of the crime and drug dealing on the estate and are determined to get the place cleaned up 'We all have children,' he said 'how shall I bring up my kids in this?'

We are joined in the Shop by Brad, the local community policeman. He is out of uniform because Judy has asked him to come with us as we go round the estate after dark. Brad is in his early thirties. Despite being white and a policeman he seems to have won the genuine trust of most residents on the estate. Almost everyone I later spoke to told me that they had completely lost trust in the police 'except, of course, Brad'.

Brad, like his colleague Paul Hurst in Toxteth, is the kind of policeman of whom we will need many more if estates like these are to throw off the terrors of lawlessness and drugs and become fit places to live in again. His weapons are not fast cars and macho attitudes, but courage and a quiet ability to communicate. His bosses like league tables of arrests, but Brad's victories come silently in the slow, patient re-establishment of trust in a community which has long ago learnt to accept that being left out is its normal lot in life.

Later that night I go out with two of Brad's colleagues, Sean and Andrew, in one of Peckham police's fast response cars. The contrast could not be sharper. Sean and Andrew's tools are their car, their radio and their speed of reaction. In the short space of two hours, we are involved in the aftermath of an armed robbery at a take-away, a car chase in which one of the other participating cars gets the 'target', a search of a suspicious vehicle and a visit to an Indian couple who have been robbed at knife point. Sean and Andrew are concerned with catching criminals, not comforting victims. So they are in and out and on to the next incident with a speed that is as bewildering as it is breathtaking. What I am seeing is the two extremes of the battle against crime at the front line.

But, as they explain to me at Peckham police station that night and next day, in both cases the police are fighting the battle without the resources, the legislation or the political support that they need to win.

The numbers in Peckham police station have recently been cut from 230 to 204. And as police strength has declined, the bureaucracy of police work has increased. Even a simple arrest for shop lifting now takes four to five hours of paperwork. Peckham station has no secretariat to type up reports, so police officers have to waste time they could be spending on the street filling in forms. And there are only two word processors, both bought from money raised by the station itself – so that the dozens of forms to be filled in for every arrest have to be done laboriously by hand.

Ironically, new legislation has made their job harder still. Crack is the big problem. Crack is not soluble in the mouth. Under the Government's Police and Criminal Evidence Act, the mouth is classified as an 'intimate orifice', which, therefore, cannot be searched. So when a crack dealer is arrested, he simply puts his wares in his mouth and the police cannot touch him.

Then there is the problem of knives. These are openly displayed and available in a local shop; wicked affairs, specially designed for human flesh. A week earlier, PC Martin Dudley had been stabbed nine times with one of these in nearby Deptford. But the police cannot stop the sale and, under the new legislation, cannot even arrest someone carrying such a knife and be confident the courts will back them.

By midnight, I am back with Judy and her husband Don in their council flat. They tell me over a glass of strong Trinidadian rum that things on these estates are slowly improving. The most optimistic conclusion I can reach is that they may be holding the slide into deprivation, lawlessness and anarchy, but it is difficult to believe that we have yet begun to reverse it.

Chapter 14

'What they were doing was imposing their solutions. What we wanted was the chance to build our own.'

8–9 February 1993

To Northern Ireland to visit an industrial regeneration programme outside Belfast and then down to Omagh, near the border, where I am shown a project designed to bring employment to a remote rural community.

♦

I am sitting in the boardroom on the old British Enkalon site, just outside Antrim, being briefed by a Dutchman who came to Northern Ireland in 1962 and has stayed here ever since, dedicating his life to creating jobs in this community.

Dr Rolof Schierbeek was the manager of the British Enkalon man-made fibre-spinning plant here when it closed in 1982. At its height, Enkalon had employed 2,900 people. Dr Schierbeek had to make the last 800 redundant when the plant finally shut. He decided then to do what he could to replace the jobs that had been lost. He persuaded the Dutch parent company, Akzo, to leave the employees' pension fund in place and appoint one of their local employees, John Wallace, to administer it. He also persuaded Akzo to continue to maintain the buildings and establish the Enkalon Foundation, a million pound charitable trust whose annual yield could be used for social and employment benefits in Northern Ireland.

Thinking of how Wills left Bristol and Tate & Lyle left Liverpool, I comment that it seems to me rather unusual for a public company to commit a million pounds of working capital to helping a community they are pulling out of. Dr Schierbeek says it is not at all unusual in Holland, where loyalty to and from the work force is more highly valued than in Britain. 'We care about the people who are made unemployed on the Continent. Management in Britain doesn't seem to care at all.'

The original plan had been to try to find a single large employer to take on the whole vast Enkalon site, which covers sixty acres. Learfan, the private jet manufacturers, expressed interest, put a down payment on the site, but then went bankrupt shortly before the deal was clinched. After four years of fruitless attempts, Dr Shierbeek decided to break the site up, using half for small business units and preserving the main production areas for a single large customer, if one could be found. Eventually, almost exclusively through Schierbeek's contacts and personal commitment, an Indonesian spinning and weaving firm, Texamaco, agreed to take over the production site. They will start off by creating 500 new jobs and hope to employ 900 when production gets going.

Dr Schierbeek tells me that, initially, he had little or no assistance from local or national politicians. He had been to see the Department of Trade and Industry who had offered some grants for small businesses, but had shown neither inclination nor interest in helping to secure a big employer. He had to work very hard to get them, eventually, to support Texamaco. Indeed, the Government had actually warned off some big employers who had shown an early interest in the site and encouraged them to look elsewhere. Dr Schierbeek explains that the Government-created Industrial Development Board (IDB) spends far too much time following the political objectives set by the politicians, rather than business objectives which would help Northern Ireland. 'The IDB will never work properly while it is the Government's creature,' he says. 'It needs to be independent.'

The local council, too, had been unhelpful to start with, but were now much more positive. One man present at my board room briefing says, 'In Northern Ireland, if it isn't capable of being used to further the cause of one or other of the sectarian interests, or one of the many sub-divisions within them, it is of no interest to the politicians.'

The rest of the huge site is fast being taken up with small businesses, including a transport firm, a taxi business, a design centre, printers, a small enamel-coating factory and a training organisation for local people with handicaps. Many of the businesses feed off each other and all will benefit when Texamaco moves in and there are 500 extra employees on site. The central site organisation has now taken on the task of advising and assisting small businesses in the tough task of surviving and prospering in the Northern Ireland economy.

We go off to visit some of the small businesses on site, including their most successful new start-up, Antrim Transformers, run by Norman Rainey.

Rainey is a remarkable businessman whose drive and energy exudes from his small stature in a way which infects everyone around him. His speech is direct to the point of bluntness which, I suspect, does not endear him to officials and bureaucrats who he thinks are getting in his way. He left school at sixteen, went into the Army and became a store keeper. When he left, five years ago, he started this business on nothing more than a lot of self-confidence and a little help from his friends, like Rolof Schierbeek. It now has a turnover of a million pounds a year.

His firm makes toroidal transformers, which are used in all hi-fi equipment. He now exports 85 per cent of his production to China, Taiwan and Japan and employs thirty-two people. 'But when I started I didn't know a toroidal transformer from a hole in the ground,' he tells me. 'I just saw a business opportunity and went for it.'

In the early days of the firm, he either hitched a lift or walked the ten miles to work every day from Ballymena where he lived in council accommodation. In the evening, he sold cosmetics in order to get enough money to live.

He was helped in the early days by a Government enterprise allowance of £40 per week, all of which he sent to his wife and children who had stayed behind in Canterbury. Apart from this, the only other assistance to which he might have been entitled was a Government grant available for firms setting up in Northern Ireland. But to be eligible for this, he had to have already obtained an investment of £50,000 from other sources. Rainey knew no one with that sort of money, so he went to see the bank. They wouldn't touch him, because he had 'no track record'.

So he was stuck. If he didn't start, he couldn't have a track record; if he didn't have a track record, he couldn't get a loan; if he didn't get a loan, he couldn't have a Government grant; if he didn't have a Government grant, he couldn't get started. Catch 22. How were small firms supposed to get off the ground?

Eventually he persuaded his bank manager to let him have a £50,000 loan on the condition that Rainey signed a secret letter saying he would never use it. So the Government's conditions were satisfied and production got going. Rainey invited an old friend and colleague, an engineer, to come over and took on six employees.

Although Rainey did not know anything about toroidal transformers, he did know exactly how to win markets – by producing quality and producing it on time. He knew that most successful manufacturers are going over to 'just in time' production, where the goods arrive at the production line just at the moment they are required, so cutting down on the working capital tied up in large stock holdings. He also knew most transformer manufacturers take an average of eighteen weeks to produce their goods, from order to delivery. He therefore decided to produce his transformers in three weeks and to make sure that their quality was higher than those of any of his competitors.

And he would do anything to get them to the customer on time, even if it cost him money on an order. He had once flown a large consignment at great expense to a customer in the Far East in order to avoid a dock strike. It had cost him dear, but it had shown the customer that he was serious about delivering on time and this had created a loyalty bond between customer and firm which was now invaluable to him.

Rainey dresses and acts exactly like all his employees and spends 90 per cent of his time on the shop floor, checking the work, advising on how to solve problems and encouraging and cajoling his work force. He tells me he could expand his operation to 500 employees and capture the world market for toroidal transformers, if only he could get the capital to increase production.

He went to the Economic Development Unit of the Northern Ireland Office for advice and assistance with increasing production and employment. But they told him that the only grants available were for help with marketing. Rainey explained that he didn't need any help with marketing as he was already selling all he could produce. More marketing would mean more orders which he didn't have the means to satisfy. Once again, Rainey finds himself caught in a Catch 22 circle, where Government assistance appears so tantalisingly close, but is always just out of reach.

The Northern Ireland Office advised him that, if he wanted to obtain capital for expansion, the best thing to do would be to look for a partner from mainland United Kingdom. But this he will not do, since it would mean losing control of the firm he has built up himself over the last five years. So he may have to move to Southern Ireland to expand, because there they give 60 per cent grants for capital expansion and corporation tax is only 20 per cent, with no tax on grants and no tax on dividends.

Referring to the rumoured £4 million grant given to Texamaco to set up in Northern Ireland, Rainey says, 'If you happen to be Indonesian, or somebody from outside, you get assistance from the Government. But they're not prepared to assist home grown business.' I tell him as I leave that, on the basis of our brief meeting, I have a feeling that a small thing like a mere Government will not be able to stand in his way for long.

I leave the Enkalon site in the late afternoon and, that evening, drive west to the border town of Omagh in County Tyrone. I notice throughout the day that there is a car full of plainclothes policemen who quietly and unobtrusively follow me wherever I go. This is an indispensable part of a politician's visit to Northern Ireland. It is a constant and silent reminder that, although things here look and seem normal, there is, behind every hedge and wall, the possibility of murder striking suddenly on a quiet country road or the corner of a city street. As we leave the outskirts of Antrim I note the headlights of my silent protector's car pull out discreetly from a lay-by and follow us on our progress west through little country towns and deserted roads towards the Irish border.

These are the roads of my youth, along which in more peaceful times I had travelled as a boy with my father on fishing expeditions. As we drove through the pretty little town of Randalstown, I get a memory of him, driving our little Standard Ten car, loaded with picnics and fishing tackle towards the nearby river Bann, which is painfully tangible.

The following day, after spending the night with two teachers, Eric and Lisa Bullick, I am taken to visit businessmen and enterprises in Omagh. I feared I would find a divided and shattered community there. This pretty and historic market town has, after all, a Catholic and Nationalist majority, an uncomfortable proximity to the Irish border, and a recent reputation of being in the teeth of the murder and violence which has so disfigured this beautiful country and its people. On our way down last night, we passed the scene of a recent massacre of employees who were in a van going home from work when they were blown to smithereens by a roadside bomb. Close by is the spot where a young friend and contemporary of my son, who often used to visit our house in Somerset, suddenly met his death with his soldier colleagues in a bus on a quiet country road on their way back from visiting their families in England.

But Omagh is not a divided, broken community. Like so much of Northern Ireland it has borne its torments with dignity and strength. This remains what it always has been; a vibrant and powerful community, with a strong voice and a clear determination of where it is going. No doubt there are the extremists and the men of violence hidden in the little country villages and the sprawling poverty of some areas of the larger towns. But those I met were ordinary people of different faiths and political beliefs, the majority of whom are more interested in the battle to strengthen their community and win jobs than in the working out of old quarrels and future dreams in their own compatriot's blood.

Men like Seamus Kerr and John Hadden, divided by their religion and their beliefs, but united in their determination to find new jobs for the little isolated and long neglected town of Carrickmore. Carrickmore (the Irish means 'Big Rock') has been a human settlement since well before the bronze age, when it was a national centre for the production of exquisite bronze implements and artifacts. Today, situated in the middle of wild, boggy country eleven miles from Omagh, the 3,000 people who live in the town and the isolated farms around suffer one of the highest levels of unemployment in rural Northern Ireland.

This is a Nationalist community and shows it. Many of the houses and lonely farmsteads that we pass fly the Irish tricolour. For many years, however, the area had elected John Hadden, who represents the non-sectarian Alliance Party, as its councillor. Until, that is, a young man called Seamus Kerr turned up and won the seat for Sinn Fein, the party's first local government victory since the foundation of the Northern Ireland state.

Seamus, though believed locally to have had close contacts with the IRA, was always perceived to have had fundamental differences with the party. Perhaps it was this that brought him in due course into conflict with Sinn Fein. Having resigned from the party mid-term, Seamus announced his intention to continue as an independent councillor. When the next council elections came around, however, for reasons perhaps best known to himself, Seamus decided to leave politics and put his considerable energies into the economic regeneration of his Carrickmore community. He then joined forces with his old political adversary, John Hadden, and others to set up a small business park in Carrickmore. But he tells me that politics is his love and some day he hopes to find his way back.

I have driven over the lonely road to Carrickmore to see John and Seamus and their colleagues. I find a bright, new modern building on the outskirts of the town. Waiting for me is the obligatory armed patrol. But inside, around a table in the modern conference room which will serve the small businesses which will be established here, the talk is of hope and reconstruction. Here are Alistair McKane from the Department of Environment, Geraldine Stafford, the centre manager, Seamus Rafferty from Omagh district council, the two centre architects, Robert Richardson and Stanley McFarlane, and Jim McGuire from the Northern Ireland Ministry of Agriculture.

Seamus and John do most of the talking. They explain that the Northern Ireland Industrial Development Board had tried, but failed, to generate economic activity here. 'They were no doubt trying to be helpful. But what they were doing was imposing their solutions. What we wanted was the chance to build our own,' John says. The present project started one night in a local pub, when a group of local people got together and decided to do something for themselves. Seamus Kerr has since visited Minnesota in the United States to see how things were done there. A plan was drawn up for a business and enterprise centre, which could also act as the base for an outreach organis- ation which would help the establishment and growth of other small businesses in the Carrickmore area.

Seamus says that one of the key tasks of the centre is to main- tain a close relationship with local schools. 'We have to change the whole culture of this area, if we are to succeed – and this means starting at the bottom, at school. The people of Carrick- more have been left out for so long that they have lost confidence in themselves. We have come to see the job of the Government as to give us things. What I want is for Government to give us the chance to do things for ourselves. There is a tradition of emigration from this area – after all there are limited opportuni- ties for those who stay in Carrickmore. Our job in this centre is to give the young people of this community something to stay for.'

The centre houses a number of units of different sizes, ranging from the very small for the first time start-up, to larger units for already established businesses. The building is now completed and 60 per cent of the available space has already been let. Funding has come equally from the Northern Ireland Depart- ment of Environment and the International Fund for Ireland, a charitable trust set up as a result of the Anglo–Irish Agreement which receives a lot of money from the United States. There is much praise from around the table for the Northern Ireland Minister then responsible for business development in the prov- ince, Richard Needham. He is credited with changing Govern- ment policy to encourage this kind of development. One of those present says, 'Most British politicians come to Northern Ireland to enhance their political careers, not to do things for Northern Ireland. Richard Needham seems to be different, he genuinely seems to want to make a difference.'

But Alistair from the Department of Environment says, 'We

are still plagued by far too many different bodies with their fingers in the pie. At present there are no less than five organisations involved in projects like this: the International Fund for Ireland, the Local Enterprise Development Unit, the Department of the Environment, the local district council and the Department of Agriculture for Northern Ireland. This leads to duplication, inefficiency and delay. What we need is a single body to which people can go for help and which is powerful enough to give a real boost to job creation and business development in areas such as these.'

Seamus tells me that they are already making plans for expansion. Near to the Carrickmore site runs a fibre optic cable called Star, laid down by British Telecom, using money provided by Europe. This could provide Carrickmore with access to inter-active, high-speed communications on a world-wide basis. Seamus has his eye on the Swedish telecottage system and similar projects operating in the South of Ireland. In these, work, chiefly of a clerical nature, is transmitted to isolated communities along the cable network system, completed in the community and then returned to the originator on the same system. Some US insurance companies are now having their claim and proposal forms dealt with in remote Southern Irish communities using inter-active fibre optic communications. Seamus says, 'For the last two hundred years – and probably more – the young people of Carrickmore have had to emigrate to places like America and Europe to find work. Now we may have the means to bring work from America to them here.'

Later in the day I will see the Star system in operation in the new business centre established in Omagh by the district council. Here they are still at the stage of testing the system and training people in its use. But they are already working with distant stations (including Paris) on maps and architects' drawings which can be displayed, discussed and amended in real time at either end.

Seamus and John make a final point before I leave. They explain that, on 1 January 1993, the European Single Market effectively destroyed the border between Northern and Southern Ireland as an economic entity. In future people will trade with whichever markets, North or South, are most available and most profitable.

Later in the day a local businessman, Protestant in his religion and Unionist in his beliefs, put it to me like this, 'Look, the fact is that I now have a choice. I can trade with Belfast to the north or Sligo to the south. And frankly, my market in Sligo is closer and often more profitable. That may not fit easily with my political beliefs, but in the end it is commercial advantage I will have to respond to. And that will increasingly take me south, not north. And if I am to work my markets effectively, I cannot be at war with them, can I? And I will tell you something else, if I want to get to European development money, I now have a choice. I can go through Dublin, or I can go through London. Frankly, Dublin is quicker, less bureaucratic and has better relationships with Brussels than London. In the end, people here will increasingly realise that, whatever history says, the present demands that we work together, rather than fight each other. In the end that single fact may give us the best opportunity we have for healing Ireland's ancient and deadly wounds.'

It is a good thought to take back to Westminster with me.

———————

Chapter 15

'Walters sell design more than we sell silk.'

15–17 February 1993

By train to Sudbury in Suffolk where I spend two days with Stephen Walters and Sons Ltd, silk weavers. I spend the first night with David Walters, who owns this family firm, and his wife Jane and the second with John and Sonia Bird, both Walters' weavers, and their son, Nick.

◆

David Walters is the eighth generation of his family to be a weaver and to run his family firm in Suffolk. He is in his late forties or early fifties, has a spare build, intelligent blue eyes and a rather quick nervous laugh which hides an extraordinary clear-thinking brain and a quiet but definite authority.

His ancestor, Joseph Walters, came to Britain with the Huguenots in the 1740s and established himself, as so many immigrants do on first coming to this country, in Spitalfields in London. A hundred years later there were 40,000 silk weavers in the Spitalfields area. But the industry suffered terribly as a result of the lifting of protective duties and the growth of the cotton industry. Unemployment and destitution were so bad amongst the weaving community that Queen Victoria herself was moved to raise special charitable funds to help them out.

In the 1870s most of the weavers who survived the 1840s recession moved out of Spitalfields to East Anglia where there was a long established wool-weaving industry. Some say they moved to get better access to water power; others because weavers' wages in the Sudbury area were lower than those in London. It was at this time that Alfred Walters moved his factory to Sudbury. There were thirty or forty established silk weavers in this area then, operating mainly from houses, or small factory premises, many of which are still visible in Sudbury today. Later in the nineteenth century, Stephen Walters moved into the present factory – no doubt in its day a model of modern factory design. The Walters have always prided themselves on keeping up with machine and product innovation; it is one of the ways they have survived when others have failed.

The great depression of the 1930s wiped out most of the remaining silk weavers in Sudbury. Today there are only three weavers left in the area. Walters survived that recession by the skin of their teeth and went on to switch production into a new product, parachute silk, just in time to exploit demand caused by the war. After the war, they switched product again and moved into making silk ties, chiefly for the club and old school market.

In the 1960s, when David Walters joined the firm, the market for school, club and 'corporate' ties was beginning to fade. By the 1970s, when he took over the firm from his father, it was clear that, like his ancestors before him, the survival of the firm and its workforce was going to depend on him finding a new outlet for their weaving skills. Since then, despite the fact that the new technologies have meant the shedding of labour in the weaving industry, the workforce at Walters has grown from seventy when David took over, to 170 today.

I have come to Sudbury to work with David and his weavers for two days because I want to see how they have converted a traditional craft industry which pre-dates Britain's industrial revolution into a modern successful firm which exports 80 per cent of their product against stiff international competition.

I am sitting with David and his management team on the first floor of their light and airy Victorian factory on the outskirts of Sudbury. We are eating a sandwich lunch and discussing the firm's position and future orders. Downstairs we can hear the muffled clatter of the weaving machines. Around me are swatches of beautifully woven silk and samples of tie designs. Further away in different rooms, separated by glass panels to maintain the sense of space and airiness, are the designers, the computers, the sales staff, secretarial and finance office of what is, for all its relatively small size, a world-wide trading firm. The conversion of this first floor has been thoughtfully done. The colour scheme is a serious dark green, and the office furniture mixes the simple modern and functional, with Victorian originals. There is something of the feel of a Laura Ashley shop about it. But the sense of purpose is unmistakable. The impression is of efficiency, individual personal service and a sense of tradition artfully mixed together. This is an effective working office. But it is also a place to bring customers to let them soak in the atmosphere of reliability, tradition, efficiency and taste.

David and his team are preparing for his forthcoming trip to America on which much of the success of next year's business and, with it, the security of the workforce's jobs will depend. It is a crucial time. Sales are not going particularly well at the moment and the current recession has made for a hard year. Each worker in Walters shares in the firm's profits every six months. In good years this has added as much as 14 per cent to their annual pay. But there had been no profit distribution this year. Indeed, David had to tell his workforce recently that the firm could only afford a small pay rise this year if they were to maintain the current level of employment.

I am astonished to discover just how much the success of the whole enterprise depends on the fashion sense of the management team and, in particular, of David himself. The bottom line depends on his ability to read the fashion market for the coming year and get it right. He tells me that this is what his predecessors have had to do to survive for three hundred years. It is also the consequence of the decision he took to change the firm's trading position when he took over in the 1970s.

At that time, the corporate tie market was in fast decline and the general tie market was being flooded by cheaper products made from manmade fibres, many coming from the developing countries whose labour costs were much lower than those in the UK. The firm simply could not survive in that market. David decided that the only way to stay in business was to move up market and graft onto the firm's high quality a design capacity which would enable them to build a new niche in the high-fashion tie market. He cleared all the production machines out of the top floor and created a much larger design department, recruiting new design talent to give him an entry into the market. 'What I had to do was to find the means to add value to our product. That was the only way to capitalise on the advantages we had over our cheaper competitors – our skill, our ability to design and our business intelligence. What you have to realise is that nowadays, Walters sell design more than we sell silk,' he says.

David's second key decision was to shift the emphasis of the firm from producing for the home market to producing for export. He knew that the firm simply could not survive on the home market – they had to become international traders, or die. Today Walters has to be prepared to both buy raw silk and sell finished products at any point around the world. Traditionally, silk weavers buy their silk from China, but at present Walters buy from Brazil, because it is cheaper. When David took over, 20 per cent of Walters' product went overseas. Today the figure is more than 80 per cent and their main markets include the United States, Europe and the Far East, especially Japan and Hong Kong.

David invested heavily, not only in human talent in the design field, but also in the new technologies. In increasingly open world markets, Walters found itself competing head to head with other producers in the field on a world-wide basis. They had to give themselves an advantage which wasn't just dependent on price. They decided to go for reliability and service to the customer.

'We had one asset in the design field to help us break into the high-fashion tie market – "the English gentleman" look. So we played to it. But we soon discovered that the "English gentleman" look means different things in the American market to what it means to the Italians. And that led us to our second change of approach – customer sensitivity. Stephen Walters has its own design "handwriting" – and that is what brings the customer to us in the first place. But in the end the whole of this organisation is dedicated to giving customers exactly what they want and being acutely sensitive to their needs. We are a totally customer-led organisation. For us, the customer is king.'

The new technologies gave them the means to achieve this. David tells me that it is now possible to meet a customer in the morning, see their proposed designs, make some agreed amendments to them, take the customer out to lunch and return afterwards to see the finished woven product.

Their major foreign competitors in the fashion tie market are the Italians, who can often produce almost to the same quality but at a cheaper price. But individual customers could never be sure with the Italians that their designs would not end up in the hands of a competitor. Much of Walters' reputation is built not just on design and quality but also on their integrity and care for customer confidentiality – which is a valuable quality, worth money to a customer who is having to operate in the extremely cut-throat fashion market.

David tells me that his most valuable asset is his workforce. He tries as far as possible to promote from within the firm and has been able to find much of the new talent he required for the shift in the firm's trading position from people who already worked at Walters. There is a single canteen and the managers and workforce join exactly the same scheme for sharing the firm's profits. They have never had a strike, though there were strong feelings about the lack of a pay rise this year. Staff turnover in the firm is low and few people belong to a union, though all are entitled to do so. When David looks for new employees what he wants to find from the education system is youngsters with a broad, not a specialised education. He says this provides the best base for learning the new skills and attitudes which are necessary to respond to the fast-changing world market.

Over dinner that night with David, his wife Jane, Walters' sales director Haley Dosser and his wife, Liz, we talk about Britain's economic position and the decline of our country's manufacturing base. Haley comments that what the country has to do to survive as an economic force is exactly what Walters' has done: move with the market, invest in our human skills, use the new technologies and rely on our entrepreneurial flare to create high value-added goods for world markets. Instead we seem to be trying to make our living in the world by selling ourselves abroad as just another low-cost production centre.

I spend the next day with the weavers, learning how the warps are laid up and how a weaving machine works. It is unbelievably delicate and skilled work that requires a very high degree of concentration and manual dexterity. It quickly becomes clear that I will never be able to earn my living as a silk weaver. But I am fascinated to see the patterns I have watched being drawn on the design room computers, emerging from the seeming chaos of threads, flying rapiers and the clatter of weaving machinery. Later I am taken to Walters' dyeing sheds to see the silk as it arrives from Brazil and China. Here it is spun off onto bobbins and dyed every colour imaginable.

And finally David arranges for me to see the new factory which he has started, weaving heavy silk furniture fabric. Here, they produce the same high quality in thick fabrics, one of which is used for bishops' gowns and retails for more than £100 a square metre.

That night I stay with John and Sonia Bird and their son, Nick. John and Sonia are both Walters' weavers, John joining the firm recently after a spell of unemployment and Sonia having worked with the firm for much of her adult life. John, near his sixties, was an orphan during the war and was adopted by a family who clearly treated him very cruelly – none of which seems to have altered his quiet Suffolk dignity and strong native sense of what is right and wrong.

I return to Westminster the following day with the thought that what Walters has done is what Britain must do; use our wits and skill to make the transition from old style traditional industry to modern leaders in an international market.

———————————

Chapter 16

'This is the end . . .'

Sign painted on the fourth floor of a block of flats at the junction of Princess Road and Moss Lane East, Moss Side, Manchester.
22–24 February 1993

North to Manchester, where I spend two and a half days living in the Moss Side area, the first night with Shamin Khan and her family and the second with Winston Simpson and his wife, Pauline.

♦

The girl is standing under a street light. Behind her is the new Manchester which is growing up around the city centre: modern office blocks, new commercial enterprises, merchant bank head-quarters – all the signs of Manchester's second growth and renewed commercial importance. This is where her clients come from. In front of her, 300 yards away, is Moss Side. This is where she lives. She tells me she is sixteen. I think she is younger. She is pretty, she is a drug addict and she is a prostitute. She says that she takes eight to ten customers a night to feed her habit and doesn't mind what she does; oral sex, anal sex, anything. She doesn't bother about condoms. She probably has three years to live.

The shocking thing about Moss Side is not just how derelict and lawless it is, but how close it is to the centre of prosperous, respectable Manchester; how easily the city lives with this foul tumour so close to its heart.

I am with Winston Simpson, one-time school drop-out, some-time youth worker and now the manager of the Nia centre on the edge of Moss Side. Winston came to England at the age of ten, when his father arrived in Britain from the West Indies. He effectively left school at fifteen, had a variety of jobs and then, after the Moss Side riots suddenly found that he had access to further education that, he says, was previously denied to Moss Side blacks, except the very bright and the very rich. He qualified as a youth and community worker and was subsequently employed with Manchester city council juvenile justice department, doing work with young offenders and children in care. He is six foot one, has a sharp natural intelligence, a disarming smile and an easy grace which seems able to defuse even the trickiest of situations.

Earlier today we had wandered around Moss Side together. Most of the great grey crescents of the Hulme flats, built in the 1960s and now being knocked down, are empty. But the sense of desolation and hopelessness spreading out from their long arms, empty walkways and cracking concrete pillars seems to invade the whole area. There is rubbish and litter everywhere, and the careful open spaces designed into these brutish shapes to bring green into trapped lives have become wastelands of desolation.

Winston calls these 'streets turned on their end' and points out 'suicide tower', named after the number of people who threw themselves out of its windows and terraces. In and out of these desolate buildings, along its aerial walkways, through its underground tunnels and in its now empty flats, flows the raw material of Moss Side's main industry – drugs. As we walk around, we can see the commerce at work.

Car loads of drug addicts, mostly white, and all with a dreadful pallor and haunted, searching eyes, cruise the estate 'to score a hit'. Many of the cars are Manchester taxis. The dealers' cars are different. They are new, smart and fast – GTis are favourites. They often come in different colours, denoting different dealing gangs. But the one thing they all have is a mobile phone – the indispensable equipment for dealer and consumer alike. It is by mobile phone that deals are made and the arrangements for delivery set up.

And in between dealer and customer are the 'mules', mostly young Afro–Caribbean boys between thirteen and sixteen, who act as couriers, messengers and lookouts. Their transport is mountain bikes, ideal for the alleys and walkways of the estate and quite impossible to catch if you are a policeman in a car. The basic uniform for mules is a tracksuit, again often in a special colour to denote your gang, a balaclava, a pair of sneakers, a loose fitting bomber jacket, a British Telecom 'bleeper' for messages and often a gun. In Moss Side, guns are said to be traded at school. Winston tells me that about 70 per cent of the young 'mules' we will see have guns and the others will be saving up to buy one. Pistols are most common. But some have sub-machine guns, the favourite being an Uzi, the deadly little automatic weapon used by the Israeli secret service. A policeman I later meet tells me how, after a recent shooting, he counted twenty-nine bullet holes in a local car. They came from a World War Two .45 calibre Thompson sub-machine gun. The youngster they suspect of using it is seventeen.

As we wander through the Moss Side shopping centre a youngster comes up to me and says, 'What the hell are you doing here – if you are not dealing fuck off!' As he does so, he pulls his bomber jacket back to reveal the butt of a sub-machine gun. Winston comes up and explains and the youngster slopes off. Winston says this boy is fifteen, well known and has been on the streets since the age of ten.

I get chatting to one of the other 'mules' at the corner of the shopping precinct. I ask him why he does it. He replies that it's the only job there is in Moss Side. He tells me that a 'mule' will be paid £50 or £60 a day just to act as a lookout. At fourteen this is big money. And the job has a career structure; he can graduate to become a dealer and have a mobile phone and a flashy car – if he lives that long.

Life for a 'mule' is always dangerous and often short. Shooting incidents in Moss Side are a regular feature of life. The police say they have two reported incidents involving guns a week. The residents say most incidents are not reported and that you can hear gun fire almost every day.

In the Moss Side shopping complex, all the banks have closed and all the supermarkets have gone. Only a stalwart greengrocer remains and a collection of smaller shops. Most are boarded up. Winston takes me to a little bakery shop, near one of the entrances. He shows me the place where a young Moss Sider called 'Dabs' had been queuing to buy a sandwich when members of a rival gang came in. He saw them coming and jumped over the bakery counter. They followed and shot him to death in front of the customers. No one has yet been convicted of the murder, but a young black man arrested and later cleared during the police investigation was later shot four times in a local pub.

More recently, Benji Stanley was gunned down inside a nearby take-away shop. He was fourteen. This, at last, so shocked the area out of its resignation that there was a protest march of mothers demanding the return of the rule of law. But it has changed nothing.

And unseen, behind Moss Side's desolate landscape and dangerous commerce, are the big dealers, the importers. They are said to be mostly Asians and some whites, who live quiet and respectable lives in the prosperous suburbs of the city. It is the young black males who are the front-line foot soldiers in this violent war which rages at the heart of one of our major cities.

Later that night, Winston and I visit Gooch Close, the home of the gang who are believed to have shot young 'Dabs' in the sandwich queue. This is a virtual no-go area for police except when they come in sufficient numbers and with proper back up. We follow one police raiding party going in to the estate. It is 1.30 a.m. and they are chasing three black youths who are driving a car which, one of the officers later tells me, 'is too flashy for them'. They corner the car in a cul-de-sac and stop two youths who they later release. But the third occupant ran off before the police could get him. The police raiding party consists of three large 'tag' vans full of police, a CID car with plainclothes officers and a smaller van with a dog and handler. After the main party has left, I get talking with one of the policemen left behind to take details.

He says 'We don't know anything about what really goes on here – we all live away from the area. We don't have any regular beat officers on the ground; we've no intelligence and no community contact. It's virtually impossible to police. Everyone carries guns, but at least they haven't used them on us yet. They just use them on each other.'

The reputation of the police in Moss Side, even amongst the law-abiding community, is disastrously low. At a Bangladeshi community and business centre in the city I heard from a group including professionals and local business men. They told me that they had stopped reporting racist incidents and attacks to the police, because they did not think it worth while any longer.

One Indian shopkeeper told me that when her shop had been raided by gunmen just before Christmas, the police had taken two and a half hours to arrive and then came on foot! A well-respected white local reporter said to me that during the Manchester riots he had seen police driving around the area in vans shouting, 'Nigger, Nigger, Nigger!' His view, reflected by others during my visit, is that 'too many in the local police force take the view that they don't need to bother much about Moss Side since it belongs to "them", and "they" should sort it out for themselves.' No doubt much of this is untrue and a lot of it is unfair. But it does indicate, at the very least, the extent to which the trust and confidence of the local Moss Side community in the police has completely broken down.

Winston takes me to the Pepper Hill estate, home of another of Moss Side's notorious drug gangs. The houses are built of pre-cast reinforced concrete and almost every other one is boarded up. Winston tells me that the council has given up cleaning the streets and doing repairs here. The Pepper Hill pub, closed and derelict, looks as though it is part of a set for a World War Two film. Apparently the area around the pub became such a centre for drug dealers and gang violence that the police and the brewery finally closed it down.

A social worker at a local community centre tells me that many of the young women in Moss Side do not have access to the wealth young men can 'earn' through the drug trade and, because of high unemployment, are denied the dignity and status that comes with having a job. Some see motherhood as a way out of this trap. A girl with no money, no chance of her own home, no role in life, no self-esteem may have a child, hoping to get these. And it seems some do. One of the sub-cultures of Moss Side, as of so many other areas in Britain where poverty is rife and opportunities have deen destroyed, is young women living with small children on benefit in council houses. Around them circle a frightening and footloose band of young men, seeking temporary relationships which will provide them with a home to live in and a share in benefits to which they are not entitled. 'Never mind what is happening to the parents; goodness knows what we are doing to children growing up largely unsupported in such an atmosphere, or what kind of problems we are storing up for the future,' the social worker says. 'It's no good the Government or others moralising about it. What this left-out generation needs is support, opportunities and guidance, not lectures. And so far we are able to give them none of these.'

Moss Side has not always been like this. During our tour, Winston and I stop at Karl Seggree's roadside tea and snack van for a cup of tea. Karl's family emigrated here in the 1950s, before they built what he refers to as 'those inhuman monstrosities', gesticulating at the Hulme flats. He describes how the area used to be full of little Victorian terraces and small corner shops: 'It was a real community, man. Then the council came along, said it was a slum and that it had to be knocked down. They never asked anyone in the area, they just moved in, compulsorily purchased what they didn't own and moved the people out. They broke up communities and they broke up families. And they were so proud of the monstrosities they put up in their place that they even named the blocks of flats after the architects that designed them! They did not even properly clear the ground before the flats were built, so the new buildings inherited their predecessors' cockroaches, mice and rats.' Karl's aunt was so heartbroken that she emigrated again, to Canada. The council is now demolishing and replacing the Hulme flats with a modern version of the low-rise high-density housing which the same council demolished thirty years ago.

Amongst the many more dramatic signs of Moss Side's physical desolation and social disintegration, it is easy to forget that this is an area of multiple problems which also suffers from all the lesser problems of poverty, social deprivation and the pressures of a multi-ethnic population.

On the first night of my visit I had stayed with Shamin Khan and her family in their little corner shop on the edge of Moss Side. The area is alive with drug dealing after dark. As with the families I had visited in Peckham, the children of Shamin's house are never allowed to go out at night, except in the direst emergencies. It was the first night of Ramadan, so Shamin, her mother Nafis, her young brother Irshad, her daughter Shahina and I were all up at 5 in the morning to eat breakfast before sunrise and start the first day of the Ramadan fast.

Shamin took me to see her friends and relatives in the area.

We called on her twin sister a few streets away. She lives with her husband and two children in what must once have been a very attractive street. 'When we came here,' she says 'things were quite different. As children, we used to be able to play on the street at any hour of the day or night. Such a thing would be unthinkable now. Now, if you drive through Moss Side, you do so with your car doors locked against gangsters with guns who break in to cars waiting at the traffic lights and rob the occupants.'

In a neighbouring street we visit a friend who has recently returned from getting married in Pakistan. She is living with her prematurely born and frail twins, little more than a few weeks old, waiting for her husband to arrive. She is living without any support and only rudimentary English, completely alone with her children above a flat which has recently been fire-bombed.

In the nearby Old Trafford Community centre, Robina Sheikh, a local community worker, explains to me that this isolation and culture clash create real problems in the Asian community. Most young second-generation Asian children have to live a life of split cultures, one in the home and one outside it. Many leave home and suicides are quite common. There is no accommodation for young people at risk locally, so many end up living in deserted flats in the Hulme crescents and quickly become enmeshed in the drug culture there. Others go to the city centre and get caught up in the vice industry.

One of the problems is the attitude of Asian men. Most want what Robina Sheikh describes as 'traditional docile' women for their wives and will arrange marriages back on the Indian sub-continent to find them. But they prefer the more liberated Asian girls of Manchester for their lovers, so many will keep a local mistress. Their wives usually know about their husbands' other women but they fear deportation if they are divorced within the first two years and anyway, being in a strange country and alien culture, are too intimidated to do much about it. Meanwhile, there being few eligible bachelors left, British Asian women looking for husbands also accept arranged marriages from 'home'. But in this case, arriving husbands expect their new brides to conform to the culture they have just left behind, rather than the more Westernised brides they find here.

Robina also tells me that there is a hidden alcohol problem

amongst many Asian men. Muslims are, of course, not permitted to drink. Nevertheless, Robina estimates that up to 50 per cent of the domestic violence in Asian families in the area is alcohol related.

The same kind of problems affect the Chinese community, as I heard when I visited the Chinese Wai Yin centre in the city. This was established in 1988 to provide help and support for Chinese women in the city. Manchester has Britain's second largest Chinese population. But, unlike the Asians, the city's Chinese community is fragmented and dispersed. Eighty-five per cent of Manchester's Chinese work in the catering trade. Most of their sons and daughters go to university and, if they can find a job, move up the wealth ladder away from their parents. In the present economic climate, however, many Chinese graduates are forced back into the family catering business. There are, I was told, two flourishing Triad gangs in Manchester making large sums from protection money paid by the Chinese catering industry.

But for Chinese women, mostly unable to speak much English, and left at home to look after their children in strange communities, the problem is isolation. The Wai Yin Centre offers them facilities for child care, English lessons, adult education courses and social contact. But it will have to close in a year's time because part funding provided for five years by the Department of Health on which it depends will soon run out.

The Bangladeshi community in the city has been more fortunate. It is much larger and has been able to set up a more or less self-funding community centre which now has thirteen staff and has been functioning for nearly ten years. The centre is run by the Bangladeshi community but opens its services to all. When I visited, there were people from a wide variety of origins there, including European, Arabic, Chinese and Asian. The centre offers child care facilities, a nursery school, training in secretarial and computer skills, business facilities, and access to a modem-operated information technology network extending across the city and beyond. They are currently opening up direct electronic mail contact with Dacca, to enable local Manchester businessmen and women to gain access to business and trading opportunities on the Indian sub-continent. And they will shortly be starting to construct a large meeting hall to be built from funds supplied jointly by the community and the city council.

Funding, of course, is the perennial problem. It will require a very large amount of money indeed to kickstart the regeneration of Moss Side and Hulme; Manchester's successful city challenge bid for the area is only the beginning of the process. Manchester city centre has had huge sums spent on it, mostly through the Development Corporation, resulting in splendid restoration and innovation only a few hundred yards away from the desolation of Moss Side and Hulme. It is said that a sum well in excess of £20 million was spent converting the Great Central Railway Station into the new G-MEX conference facility. Not surprisingly, Moss Siders I speak to are adamant about the need for their community to enjoy a fair share of any jobs and money which might accompany the British bid to have the Olympics staged in the city. They fear that, as so often in the past, prosperous middle-class parts of Manchester will be the main beneficiaries.

A few years ago, some West Indian community leaders decided that they couldn't wait for the council and the Government any longer. So they started doing things for themselves. They set up the Carriocca organisation. At first they concentrated on provid-ing training for West Indian youngsters in the Moss Side area. But when the youngsters were trained, there were still no jobs available for them. So they set up Carriocca Enterprises, the first enterprise centre designed to help West Indians get into business. 'Knowing how the system works, we decided to make it work for us,' Betty Luckhom, Carriocca's company secretary tells me. The Carriocca Enterprises complex now occupies smart modern premises which provides work space for small businesses on a four and a half acre prime site not far from Moss Side. But those who have set it up describe the long battle they had to fight with the city council to get it established. Stanley Butcher, Carriocca's manager, says, 'In order to win, we blacks had to learn to lobby and fight on an equal basis with them. They didn't think we should have this site – they told us it was too good for us. They kept on saying things like "Are you sure you West Indians can handle a project as complicated as this?" They tried to set us up to fail – but we didn't. We had to hire and brief our own archi-tects. We had to learn how to write a business plan and assess the value and potential of a site. But we soon learnt. And now we have a new building on a great site and it's 85 per cent occupied with small businesses. And what we have done has raised the value of the whole area. When we came here this was wasteland. Now McDonalds have just bought the site next door and a major food distribution company is coming soon, too.'

In nearby Cheetham Hill, a black resource centre has been established. Its organiser, Robert Jones, tells me that the council has done everything it can to close them down, asking a rent four times that paid by a nearby, predominantly white community centre and then, at the last minute, raising the selling price above the valuation agreed for sale just when the centre had found the money to buy its building. But so far they have kept going.

And now the Moss Side and Hulme Community Development Trust is moving in to regenerate the whole area. Winston is a trustee and took me to their open day. They showed me the plans for the new estate they will build on the site of the Hulme flats – they are impressive. But I did not yet see the sense of local ownership of the project by the local community that will be necessary to convince Moss Side that this is not just another bunch of experts coming in from the outside to tell them what to do.

And I noticed that most of the labour to knock down the flats and build a new community was not coming from the Moss Side and Hulme communities, but from outside. I spoke to twenty-three young Moss Siders, black and white, being trained by the trust in building skills. Only two have been given jobs building the new Moss Side they will be living in. Even clearing the rubble before the new community trust offices were built was done by a firm brought in from outside.

The decent, committed and courageous people whom I met in Moss Side and Hulme have paid a high enough price in the past for outsiders who think they know best. I left hoping that we are not about to make the same terrible mistake again.

Chapter 17
Wet oilskins and room service

1–3 March 1993

To Padstow to join Mike Hosking and the crew of the Silver Harvester *for two days and nights beam trawling in the Irish Sea.*

◆

The little trawler bucks and pitches its way into the sea which surges black and heaving around us and sometimes over onto the deck where we are working. Beyond the tight circle of the ship's lights, a bright crescent moon is shot to tiny reflected shards on the surface of a choppy sea. Above the crash of the ship's bows butting into the waves and the throb of the engines beneath my feet, the two thick wire hawsers drawing up the heavy nets from the sea bed forty-five fathoms below sing and crack on the winch. It is 3.30 on a blustery and bitter morning, thirty miles north of Trevose Head in the Irish Sea. The wind is bitingly cold and blowing force five or six from the north east and we are pulling up our third 'haul' of the night on the beam trawler *Silver Harvester.*

A few minutes ago, our skipper Del Puckey slackened the *Silver Harvester*'s speed, flicked on her deck lights and swung her head away from the north-westerly course he had been steering, into the wind and sea. Down below the three of us who will lift this 'haul' end a fitful hour's sleep and blearily pull on damp oilskins and boots before going out on deck to meet the wind and spray and start our work.

For the last three hours, *Silver Harvester* has been trawling two huge nets along the sea bottom on a course which Del Puckey calculates will give us the best chance of netting fish, without snagging the wrecks and rocks which dot this part of the Irish Sea. Each net weighs the best part of three tons and is dragged along the sea bed at the end of over 200 metres of wire hawser, suspended from two large beams swung out from the ship's side. The underside of the net is made up of heavy chain and works on the same principle as a farmer's harrow on the sea bottom. As the ship moves forward the chains disturb bottom-feeding fish such as plaice, sole and monk fish, who swim up and are trapped in the open jaws of the net and then pushed back down its tunnel to the tightly meshed 'cod end', where they remain until drawn up at the end of the 'run'.

Each 'run' is plotted in the *Silver Harvester*'s darkened bridge house on their satellite-controlled terrestrial navigation system. Del is able, even in the worst weather, to calculate with very great accuracy not only where he is but what previous runs he has done and where the hazards are. This accuracy is important for safe and effective fishing. A snagged net and an unalert skipper have been known to drag a beam trawler over.

Out on deck, the hawsers (known as warps) pull slowly out of the black sea into the pool of light around the ship. Each hundred metres of warp is marked so that the winch operator knows how much there is still to go. As I watch, the sea suddenly breaks into a surge of froth as the net mouth, held open by a heavy beam, comes to the surface. There are two large iron shoes at either end of each net beam which hold it to the bottom when fishing. As the nets are raised out of the water, these swing about wildly with the roll of the ship, crashing against the guard rails around which we are working. This is a moment when an unwary hand or arm caught over the guard rail could result in a lost limb. Brad Smart, who has been working the winch, comes to help me as we both lean over the side of the ship to attach a cable to a line leading to the cod end, now lying in the water along the ship's side and plainly identifiable by the orange rope trailer which protects it from chafing on the sea bottom. Del, in the wheel house, brings the ship almost to a dead stop, holding her head into the wind. A few more moment's work with the winch and the cod end is brought up, full of fish, swung with the roll of the ship over the working deck and lowered. Brad and I go forward and he grabs the end with one hand and, with a small mallet, knocks away the chock which closes the cod end bottom. About half a ton of fish, crabs, shells and rocks land with a thump on the wooden deck. It is now my job to go up inside the opened net and pull out the valuable sole which are trapped by their gills in its mesh. This would be a wet and unpleasant job even in a flat calm sea. It is an extremely uncomfortable one with the net swinging about, my feet slipping on the pitching deck and the rasping skin of wriggling cat fish, also caught in the net, slapping against my face.

When the net is empty, it is closed again and the steel wedge banged in to hold it shut. Catching the roll of the ship, we swing the net out over the side and lower it back into the water. Then, with the ship steering a steady course, Del gives a short blast on the hooter. This is the signal for us simultaneously to drop both nets, swiftly but precisely into the water and astern of the ship, avoiding, at all costs, catching them in the ship's turning propellers (something we failed to do on one occasion, at the cost of a good deal of lost fishing time and £700 worth of net, including the cod head). This is a moment when an unwary foot caught in a cable as the net pays out can whisk a person over the side. Russ, the mate, remarks that you would last about four minutes in this sea and temperature.

With the nets safely streaming astern of the *Silver Harvester* and making their way back to the sea bed, we turn our attention to the fish now lying in a muddy heap on the deck. The pile we have drawn up from the sea bed includes old boots, rocks, shells, star fish, rubbish ditched from previous ships in passage and, of course, the fish that give the *Silver Harvester* its living. The job now is to sort them out. In the midships of the boat are two sets of four baskets into which the fish are thrown. One is for round fish (cod, hake, whiting and pout). The second is for flat fish (lemon and megrim sole, plaice, brill, dabs and turbot). The third is for monk fish, some three or four feet long, with mouths as wide as their huge bodies and teeth sharp enough to go through a sea boot if you allow them to snap their powerful jaws shut on an unwary foot. The last basket is for sole, dark and muddy green as the sea bottom, which are our most prized and valuable catch. There are also separate baskets in the midships area for octopuses, squid, scallops and gurnards which are red, spiky and used for cat food.

Occasionally we find a weaver fish or two. These come up from the sea bed coloured bright green, turquoise and blue. But they have a vicious spine which can go through a glove and poison an arm very painfully. Brad points out one type of weaver, which looks to my unpractised eye just like any other round fish, but apparently contains a sting poisonous enough to put an adult in hospital for a few days.

When we have sorted the takeable fish into the baskets I open small metal trap doors in the sides of the guard rail and, using a combination of a high pressure sea water hose and an implement like an over-grown kitchen squeegee mop, push what is left back out to the sea. This causes great delight amongst the gulls which permanently accompany us. The waves which have been constantly breaking over the deck and surging around our feet as we work help wash out the left overs. By my calculation, I push over the side a weight of fish equal to that we have put into the baskets. But they are all too small or of a kind we are not allowed to take. All these fish will die because their swim bladders will have been burst by the release of pressure as they were drawn to the surface from the sea bottom. But the laws passed by Parliament in the name of conservation say that, whether they die or not, the *Silver Harvester* cannot bring them to shore for human consumption. They must be left at sea to be food for the gulls or to rot on the sea bottom and pollute it.

We now get down to the final task of the haul, gutting the catch. The three of us gather at a table under the fo'c'sle, with the waves crashing over our heads and, basket by basket, gut and clean the fish. This is a job for sharp knives, a swift hand and a good deal of manual dexterity – not always the easiest thing to manage while keeping a footing on a deck awash with waves heaving and bucking beneath you. I have not yet got the hang of it, but I notice that my three mates, Brad, Quentin and Russ, manage it with extraordinary speed while keeping up a good-natured banter, much of it at my expense. My hands are too cold and my brain is too numb at this time of the morning to be able to match them in either wit or speed.

Afterwards I wash down the decks again to get rid of the fish heads and innards and we lower the baskets full of cleaned and sorted fish into the *Silver Harvester*'s refrigerated hold where they are iced, stacked and secured. Then back to the fugginess of the after cabin, where I pull off even wetter oil skins, gulp down a cup of steaming hot tea and collapse on a bunk to sleep, fully clothed, until the next haul in an hour or so's time. The *Silver Harvester* has four deck hands, and each haul requires three people. So each person does two hauls on and one off, in a non-stop rotation throughout the six or seven-day voyage.

I joined the *Silver Harvester* three hauls and fourteen hours ago as she swung at anchor under the lee of Polzeath Head at the mouth of Padstow harbour. She is not a beautiful ship. But she is a sturdy and workmanlike one. Mike Hosking, her owner, met me at Padstow quay and on this blustery, cold but bright March day took me out to the *Harvester* on a small inshore fishing boat, operated by a friend. As we clambered on board, he introduced me to her crew. Del Puckey, the skipper, Dale, his son, Russ Pauley, the mate, Quentin Bates, Andy Hayes, Brad Smart and finally Tim Oswald, the *Silver Harvester*'s irrepressible chef, whose shout of 'room service' always preceded the most welcome sight of my two days at sea – that of Tim carrying a seemingly impossible number of full cups of tea, completely unaffected by, the rearing and heaving deck on which he was standing.

Mike Hosking owns two other boats fishing out of Cornish ports. Both are smaller than the *Silver Harvester*. One, commanded by his son Jeremy, is at sea at the same time as us, a hundred miles to the south west near the Bishop's Rock light.

Mike is a Cornishman to the marrow of his bones – large, bluff, perhaps a little too round in his girth, but with an infectious smile and a ready joke that makes him excellent company. Behind the bluff exterior, however, there is a sharp and questing mind and a strong business sense. He is the fourth generation of his family to have earned their living from the sea around the coasts of Cornwall. His father fished for lobsters and Mike joined him at the age of fifteen, leaving school a year later. His early years were spent fishing for lobsters in a tiny boat when the weather was good and making the willow pots which were the tools of his trade when it was not. Lobster and inshore fishing is an arduous and dangerous occupation – in the last year alone the port of Padstow has lost five young men earning their living from inshore fishing.

In the 1950s Mike's father decided to buy a thirty-three-foot wooden vessel called the *Provider* to maintain the family income. He calculated that the knowledge they had gained through shell fishing with pots, hand-line fishing for mackerel, and driftnetting for pilchards in local waters would enable him to branch out into the pelagic fishing industry (i.e. netting fish that swim in shoals, such as herring, pilchard, mackerel and sprat). Mike went to Brixham in Devon to learn about pelagic fishing and then became, with his father, the first Cornish fisherman to undertake this type of fishing from a Cornish port in Cornish waters. His first vessel was a wooden ship. It soon became obvious however that a larger, steel vessel was required. In 1975 his second boat, the *Daugeeny*, was built for him in Aberdeen, and in 1978 he bought the *Silver Harvester*, an ex-Dutch beam trawler, which had been modified and lengthened by twelve foot for greater capacity. In 1981 Mike's brother was killed on the *Silver Harvester*, when the tackle on a mast-head pulley broke under the weight of a heavy catch.

They had ten good years of pelagic fishing. Many other Cornish fishermen followed Mike and his father and the Cornish fishing fleet was completely refurbished on the proceeds. At the height of the boom, there were twenty pelagic boats operating out of Cornish and Devon ports. And new jobs were created onshore as well – it is calculated that there are thirty-five fishing related jobs on shore for every fisherman there is at sea. Canneries and fish factories employing nearly a thousand people were set up to serve the Cornish pelagic catch.

Then the Scots came down. And the French. And the Spanish. And soon the waters became fished out and the stocks, especially of mackerel, dropped alarmingly. The European Community began to introduce new conservation measures. A 'mackerel box' was drawn up to cover an area from Portland to Cherbourg, to the Scillies, to Dublin, to Fishguard. Inside it was illegal to take mackerel. Mackerel fishing was permitted beyond the box but greatly reduced quotas were introduced. Mike used to land 2 to 3,000 tons of mackerel, but was now given a quota of 250 tons a year. Almost overnight, 80 per cent of the shore-based fishing industries were wiped out and today, from the twenty vessels once engaged in pelagic fishing from Cornish ports, there remain only two.

But of course pelagic fishing for other varieties, principally pilchard, continues and the nets still bring in mackerel from Cornish waters. A 15 per cent catch of mackerel is allowed when fishing for other species. Anything over has to be returned to the sea. These fish are dead by the time they reach the surface. But they may not be landed; they must be thrown back. Mike recalls one time when he accidentally hauled a full net comprising around forty tons of mackerel. He kept the net astern of the boat while he contacted the Ministry people ashore and asked if he could land his catch, sell it and give the money to charity, rather than let the fish return dead to the sea bed. He was refused.

He believes, nevertheless, that the mackerel stocks have now recouped their strength and that a limited return to mackerel fishing in the box is possible.

In the mid 1980s, many West Country fishermen decided to get out of pelagic fishing and extend beam trawling for bottom fish to an all-year-round operation.

But now they will have to cope with a fresh problem; the new Sea Fish Conservation Bill which we have just passed through Parliament. Mike believes that this piece of legislation will prove dangerous, unworkable and extremely damaging to the British and Cornish fishing industry. Under the new regulations French fishermen will have the right to lift more fish out of Cornish waters than Cornish fishermen will be able to take. The French quota for cod, for instance, is 13,380 tons in the box which includes the Cornish coast, whereas Britain's quota is only 1,450 tons.

Overall Britain's quota of fish in the Channel and Irish Sea areas is approximately 12 per cent of vulnerable species, whereas other European nations can lift 88 per cent of the fish from what our fishermen regard as 'our' waters.

But the real damage will come with the Government's imposed 'days at sea' regulations. Under these, individual boats will be limited to a set number of days at sea, based on the number of days they spent at sea in 1991. Britain is the only European nation that has decided to limit its fishermen in this manner. So, while

Cornish fishermen are being forced to sit in port, their French competitors will be able to continue fishing their waters.

What will make this legislation dangerous as well as unfair is the fact that British fishermen must stay in port for a continuous stretch of a given number of days at a time. Once they have chosen the days they have no flexibility. And, of course, they have no control over the weather in the remaining days in which they are able to go to sea. So a fisherman who has, say, an allocation of 320 days at sea and who has already spent his forty-five days in port, must be prepared to go to sea whatever the prevailing weather conditions in his remaining eligible days in order to cover costs. Given the mortgages still outstanding on many of the younger fishermen's boats and the difficulties of the current economic climate, Mike is in no doubt that some fishermen's lives will be put at risk because they will have to put to sea and try to fish in weather which is too treacherous for safe fishing.

Mike tells me that most Cornish fishermen readily accept the need for conservation – after all the long-term survival of their livelihood depends on maintaining fish stocks. But a better way to conserve stocks would be to establish boxes around the fish-breeding areas which would be closed to all fishing by all nations for the periods when the fish breed every year. This would prevent the kind of wastage I saw in having to put back fish which were already dead, but undersize. They have proposed this alternative to the Government, but no one seems to want to listen.

At the end of my two days at sea, we put back into Padstow to learn that overnight, forty miles to the north of where we were fishing, a Cornish trawler has been lost. The crew were lucky; they were winched to safety by an RAF helicopter.

By the time I leave I have sufficiently got the hang of how to do a 'haul' not to get in the way. I have hands which are chapped and cut, have had so little sleep that I can barely think straight and have a deep respect for those who choose to win their living from the sea. My companions, of course, go straight back to the fishing grounds: they have another five days uninterrupted fishing to do. I shall remember the comradeship, teamwork and unobtrusive care for my safety that these eight men have shown me over the last two days and nights. And I shall especially remember the taste of Tim Oswald's breadcrumbed plaice eaten at 5 in the morning, ten minutes after I had untangled it from the inside of a beam trawler's cod end. I suspect no other fish I shall eat will taste quite like it!

Chapter 18

'We are the first bairns to be able to communicate with our fellow bairns on a daily basis and we're very lucky.'

8–10 March 1993

North to Aberdeen and then on by propeller-driven aircraft to Kirkwall on Orkney. Spend the morning in Kirkwall Grammar School on Orkney and then across Orkney Sound by ferry to Hoy. Spend the night with Leslye and John Budge.

◆

The big ferry, carrying a petrol tanker, three or four private cars and a van, swings out of the confined waters of Houton Bay, into Orkney Sound and heads for the distant island of Flotta. I am the only foot passenger on board.

It is a beautiful, bright and almost cloudless day. As we leave the narrow entrance of Houton, there are cormorants diving along the shallow waters of the shore line, a grebe paddling purposefully out to sea and a pair of mallards flying low and close to the ship. Further out across the Sound, a flight of dunlin skimming low over the water show their white undersides like a flash of sunlight as they turn. In the distance, the low-slung, green hills of Orkney throw their protective arms around the sound, sparkling and blue. And beyond again, down the Pentland Firth, I can see more distant islands, edged with black where shallow cliffs come down to the sea, each dotted with distant white houses, the remains of two hundred years of war defences and lighthouses marking the most dangerous promontories.

These islands lie green and low, as though seeking to offer the least resistance to the winds which so constantly blow across them. Only Hoy, where we are headed, rises high and black with heather above the sea, its thousand-foot cliffs falling sheer into the surging waves at the western edge of the island.

In the deep clear water under us as we pass across the Sound lies an entire German battle fleet, scuttled here by their crews at the end of World War One. And to the north, a little further away rest the remains of the *Royal Oak* and many of her crew, sunk by a German U-boat which, with extraordinary daring, slipped past the sea defences and into these confined waters to torpedo her in the opening months of World War Two. These waters are accustomed to war. They were used by the Vikings to gather their raiding parties for Scotland. They were used to assemble convoys heading for America to relieve the beleaguered British forces during the American War of Independence. Later, the Hudson Bay Company's vessels gathered here before making the journey across the Atlantic to northern Canada and merchantmen collected here for protection from the French during the Napoleonic wars.

Our ferry calls first at Flotta, where they refine the North Sea oil which is today the chief source of wealth for Orkney, and then makes the short crossing to the old admiralty pier at Lyness on the island of Hoy. I have come to Hoy to look at one of Britain's first 'Telecottages'. Telecottages were first established in the remote villages of Northern Sweden in the early 1980s by a Dane, Henning Albrechson. The idea was to equip a single house, or village hall, with computers, faxes and electronic communications which are open to the whole community, so as to enable individuals to use and market their personal skills to the outside world. The Telecottage movement is now well developed, especially in Scandinavian countries, and has already done much to maintain the viability of remote communities which would otherwise have withered.

The Hoy Telecottage is run by Lydia Hardcastle, who meets me off the ferry at Lyness. Lydia is from Manchester, but like so many who have settled on these islands, came here for a holiday and decided to stay. As she drives me up through Lyness in her battered old car (cars on Hoy need neither licenses nor an MOT as there is only one road on the island), Lydia reminds me that on this island there used to live and work between 40 and 50,000 people. The remains of the old naval base, so vital to Britain's maritime control of these northern seas, lie all around me. One or two World War Two brick buildings still survive, including the old forces cinema, now converted into an imposing and spacious private house. But mostly the island is slowly reclaiming these latest intruders to its peace. Moss, heather and the short clumpy Hoy grass is growing over the concrete plinths on which, only fifty years ago, stood buildings, machine shops and the guns which protected the base from sea and air.

Today the population of Hoy is 440, about half of whom are 'incomers', like Lydia. There are many who come to the islands of Orkney seeking some romantic notion of self-sufficiency and living close to nature. Often they arrive from inner cities determined to instruct the people of Orkney how to live their lives. Mostly, they do not last long. Having come to seek nature, they soon discover the inconvenient fact that they cannot alter nature to make it more convenient. The way the Orcadians have learnt to live with the land and the sea is the only way it can be done. In the end the constant wind, the hard, wet winter and the isolation drive them, often painfully, back to where they came from. But some come here, love the islands of Orkney for what they are, accept their terms and stay.

Lydia has suggested that before we start work she should take me to Rackwick Bay on the south-western edge of the Island. As we drive on the single road up from the green low land around Lyness and into the black heather-covered mountains on the western half of the island, she tells me why she came here and stayed. 'There is no crime on the island, our kids can run wild and free, the way we used to in the old days; you don't have to worry about them running on the hills; there is no danger from traffic, we never have to lock our cars or our houses. Yes, the winters are tough, the wind seems to blow for months on end and the weather is never particularly welcoming except for about ten or fifteen days a year. But there is a wonderfully strong sense of community here and if that and peace is what you want from life, then the price is worth paying, isn't it?'

We arrive at Rackwick bay just as the dusk is beginning to fall. The Atlantic surge thunders on the beach, throwing up spray which diffuses the low, yellow light of the sun. Behind us, huddled along the bay's edge in its niche between the towering cliffs, lie the few houses of what used to be a small fishing and farming village. Many are now deserted. High on the hill above us, Lydia points out the dimly glowing light in the little cottage of the composer Sir Peter Maxwell Davis. I can understand why they both want to live here.

We drive back across the island to the home of Leslye and John Budge and their two children, Helen, aged five and crowned with a crop of glorious golden hair and Matthew, six, currently rather toothless and, as I am later to find to my cost, a master of Connect 4, at which he beats me regularly and roundly. John is a local Orcadian who farms beef on the south part of the island. He is also a fireman, lifeboatman, leader of the local band, head of the local masonic organisation and part-time machinery contractor. Leslye, like Lydia, comes originally, from Manchester.

Later in the evening we are joined by Mairhi Tricket, Hoy's local councillor, Terry Thomson, who seems to have a finger in every Hoy pie, Ann Sutherland, the wife of a farmer and an accomplished designer, Moira Groat, part-time teacher, Julie Thompson, local agent for the National Farmers' Union and her husband Stanley, who farms sheep and enlivens our conversation with a dry, sharp wit for which he is famous.

The conversation is of Hoy and Orkney and its problems, of falling populations and the difficulties caused, even to these robust and self-contained people, by rural isolation. Mairhi tells me about the neighbouring island of Graemsay, population twenty-seven, no regular ferry service and a school with only five pupils. Like the children from every other island with a small school population, the children of Graemsay will go to secondary school on 'mainland' Orkney at the age of twelve. For most it will be the first time they have been off the island without their parents. They will live all week in hostels at Kirkwall and return home only at weekends.

In Hoy there is a primary and a secondary school. But there is now a real threat that the secondary school will be closed down as it is proving prohibitively expensive to the Local Education Authority. Mairhi fears that, if the secondary school closes, there will be a further depopulation of the island. Even those who were born and bred here will not want to stay if they have to be parted from their children.

Then there is the problem of employment. At present the main industry on the island, after agriculture, is fish farming. But this is very vulnerable to changes in the business climate and is currently going through hard times. Some years ago Highlands and Islands Enterprise tried to set up a co-operative on the island. They threw a lot of money at it at the start, but never provided it with the continuing support it needed. So now the organisation has declined and runs only a local café for tourists during the summer and a freight service for the island.

I ask for a list of facilities on the island. Stanley Thomson says, 'A café open in the summer; two and a half pubs [the half only opens in the summer]; a part-time museum about World War Two; two shops; an occasional prostitute who is balding; a swimming pool for those brave enough to use it and some all weather tennis courts.'

In the course of our conversation it became apparent that most of the organising on Hoy is done by the women. Ann Sutherland, an Orcadian born and bred, tells me that this is an old Orcadian tradition. In the past the island communities relied heavily on fishing, and with the men folk absent for long periods at sea it fell to the women to organise things in the community and carry, largely alone, the burdens of bringing up the children.

It also becomes clear just how important to the lives of these people and their community Lydia's Telecottage facilities have become. Julie Thompson uses it for wordprocessing and producing NFU leaflets. Moira Groat, who chairs the Telecottage organisation, joined Leslye Budge in using Hoy school's distance-learning facilities to master book-keeping and now does all the farm accounts on the Telecottage computers. Ann Sutherland's art working and design skills are used to produce brochures for local businesses and tourists, using the Telecottage's desk-top publishing programmes.

The next day, Lydia takes me to the Telecottage, housed in the old village school building. Inside I meet Jude Callister who, with Lydia, runs the organisation. The facility consists of a single room in which are two computers equipped with word processing, spread sheet and desk-top publishing programmes, a fax, a photocopier, a full range of secretarial equipment and modem communications linked into the British Telecom national network.

Since its establishment, the Telecottage has acted as a focal point, bringing together the human talent of the island. Using local people's skills, this remote island community is able to offer corporate image design, annual report production, graphic design illustration, brochure and leaflet production, translation services into German, French and Spanish and general small business support. Their current customers include the Orkney Islands council, local arts and community groups on other islands, the Church of Scotland, the European Community and a Third World charity.

The Telecottage, whose facilities are open to anyone on the island, either through an annual membership fee or by paying for each use, was established in 1990 on a grant of £33,000 for a three-year period from Highlands and Islands Enterprise. This was backed up by a further donation of £20,000 worth of equipment from British Telecom. At the end of the three-year period, the Telecottage is expected to be self-funding. Lydia tells me that Highland and Island Enterprise did not expect them to be able to succeed because it considered the community on Hoy too small. But she is now fairly confident that the islanders would prove them wrong and that the Telecottage would be self funding by the end of the grant period.

During the morning, a constant stream of islanders flow in and out of the office. Anna Geerdes, Dutch and married to a Scottish eel fisherman, comes in to photocopy some music scores for a local music group. Fiona Summerville wants to produce a brochure for the self-catering flats she is opening up for tourists in the outbuildings of her lighthouse home. She also sews and makes candles and uses the Telecottage facilities to help her with her PR and packaging. Graham Monteith, the minister for Hoy and Flotta, does some church notices and tells me that the Telecottage has become a sort of community hall and is invaluable, not only as a means through which locals in this isolated community can make commercial use of their skills in a wider market, but also as a resource which enables community activity on the island. Judith, an artist who does exquisite bird pictures, markets these through the Telecottage. Roy Harris is doing some research into farming and conservancy for the Nature Conservancy Council and the European Community and makes extensive use of the computers for data management and communication with his customers.

What the Hoy Telecottage now desperately needs is more markets off the island, which they can service using their on-line communications system. Similar Telecottage facilities have been established on other Orkney and Shetland islands and form the beginning of an island network which could bring together and market talent on an even wider basis. On the island of Unst, off Shetland, they have a particularly active Telecottage network, with two separated out-workers communicating on telephone lines from two even more isolated islands.

But not everyone chooses to use the common facilities offered by Telecottages; some have set up their own private systems. One man on the Orkney 'mainland' manages the flow of sea traffic around the port of Hong Kong from computers in his cottage overlooking Orkney Sound. Another couple on Orkney analyse and distribute 'recipes' for solving problems in the oil industry to customers around the world.

Lydia explains that this is all part of a powerful and growing world-wide 'telecommuting' network. Many big firms are now finding that it is cheaper and more effective to use modern communications systems to take work to people, rather than take people along increasingly crowded transport systems to increasingly expensive central office facilities.

Rank Xerox, a pioneer in this field, estimates that more is spent on the cost of central facilities in many modern firms than is spent on the salaries for their work force. Pacific Bell in the US has been telecommuting since 1984 and found productivity has gone up by 20 per cent because its telecommuters have been able to work in more congenial surroundings and in a flexible manner more suitable to their lifestyle and family commitments. In Germany, TV licence applications are now processed by a teleworking network employing only disabled people.

At midday, Lydia takes me down to the local school, a bright, modern building where there are thirty-three children between the ages of four and fourteen on the roll. Hoy school is linked to other Orkney island schools on a computer-communications-based 'white board' system. This system uses British Telecom telephone lines for voice and visual communication to enable a teacher to teach a class at two or more distant outstations in the same way as in a single classroom. It enables a lesson to be conducted simultaneously over a wide variety of locations and combines the advantage of distance learning with the benefits of personal instruction.

On the previous day, in Kirkwall Grammar, I saw this system in operation, when I took part in a lesson on coastal navigation (a vital and life-saving subject in this dispersed island community), given by a teacher in Stromness, twenty miles away, to four primary school pupils on remote Papa Westray island, forty miles to the north. I sat, like others taking the lesson, at a table with a loud speaker and microphone system connecting all those involved. In front of me in the classroom in Kirkwall is a large television set on which the lines drawn by the teacher or participating pupil appear. On the table is a small white board and electronic pencils capable of making different coloured marks on the TV screens which we could all, in our separate locations, see. The teacher conducts the lesson using the 'white board' system exactly as he would a blackboard, asking his distant and invisible pupils to participate by drawing their own lines on the board in answer to questions. Shortly, new video phones will arrive and teacher and class will be able to see each other as well.

Forty miles away on Papa Westray my fellow pupils are Joel, aged eleven, Gary, seven, Stuart, seven and Jonathan, ten. Jonathan tells me that he thinks the system is 'great'. Previously Papa Westray primary children were completely cut off from the school colleagues they would meet when they went to secondary school on the Orkney 'mainland'. Jonathan tells me, 'We are the first bairns to be able to communicate with our fellow bairns on a daily basis and we're very lucky.'

Christine Hopkins is the primary school teacher at Papa Westray. She tells me the 'white board' system has enabled her to offer curricular services to her four pupils which would otherwise never have been available. And it is cheaper, too. The telephone lines cost £18.60 per hour, in comparison to the £50 per visit the Education Authority has to pay for a peripatetic teacher to fly to an outlying island. Christine tells me that pupils take to the system easily, since every youngster nowadays has been brought up with television and expects entertainment and enjoyment to come from it. But the biggest advantage of the system, I am told by Stuart's mother, who is also participating in the lesson, is in the contact which it provides for children in remote island communities with their peers elsewhere. Leaving a small island like Papa Westray at the age of twelve to go to Kirkwall Grammar can be a very disturbing experience. The 'white board' system has given them regular contact with their future school mates and this has led to a big improvement in confidence and communication skills amongst the Papa Westray children. And, of course, the system can be used for adult education too. This is the way Leslye Budge had learnt her book keeping on Hoy. Christine tells me that every small rural school in Britain could benefit from the 'white board' system. 'It might keep a few more from being closed.' The teacher from Stromness points out that using this system also has the advantage of preventing over-domination by the centres. Instead of always being dependant on the local big town or city, each school is able to develop its own strengths which it can then 'export' to the others. For instance, the coastal navigation lesson which we are now doing was developed in Stromness, but has been taught from there as far down as Kinlochbervie, in Sutherland on the Scottish mainland.

Returning on the ferry to the Orkney mainland, I am invited onto the bridge to speak to the captain, a big Orcadian who tells me he has spent a life at sea, most of it away from the islands. He reminds me that these islands have a civilisation which is more than 3,000 years old. People settled here because Orkney was a centre of communication in the days when the sea was the only means of travel for goods and people. Communications has always been the key to survival and prosperity in this area – and, in its most modern form, remains so.

Chapter 19

'We will be in real trouble when even your doctor doesn't understand.'

15–16 March 1993

To Oxford to meet and stay with members of Oxford's gay and lesbian community. Spend the day with OXAIDS and the Oxford Gay and Lesbian Centre and in the evening, stay with Lis Burch.

◆

Elaine is in her late forties. She was a nurse in a bustling Hampshire hospital. One day several years ago, she heard her fellow nurses joking and laughing about a lesbian patient in one of the wards. Elaine said 'We are not all that bad, you know.'

Within four hours she was called in by the hospital authorities and given a month's notice to leave her nurse's accommodation. The hospital administrator said to her 'I don't want you to think we are on a witch hunt, but there are eighteen and nineteen-year-old girls here and we are responsible for all of them. We just cannot have you living in the same accommodation. If it came to light there would be hell to pay.'

The accommodation was single sex but no one objected to men staying the night. Ninety-seven per cent of all sexual assaults are carried out by heterosexual males, 2.5 per cent are carried out by homosexual men and 0.5 per cent are carried out by heterosexual women. There is no known case of a sexual assault being carried out by a lesbian.

Elaine was working at the time on a female surgical ward. When she arrived for work next day she noticed that the small windows between the sister's office and the room where patients are made ready for operations had been newly whitewashed. About a year later, she learned that a small square had been scraped in the pane through which she could be observed from the office when left alone with a female patient, and that other nurses were secretly put on a rota to keep a watch on her. A few days later, Elaine was also told that she was now considered unsuitable to work on the children's ward. There are no known instances of lesbian assaults on children. Ninety-eight per cent of sexual assaults on children are by heterosexual men.

Over the next few weeks, Elaine received a number of threatening and abusive poison pen letters, had obscene graffiti painted on her door, had her car tyres slashed and her car bodywork sprayed with paint.

I am sitting with Elaine in the Oxford Gay and Lesbian Centre, a brightly renovated and preserved old church hall which is one of Britain's only gay and lesbian community facilities. The centre was opened after a long battle with some on Oxford city council and other 'informed' Oxford opinion, in 1989. With me are Lis, who has organised this trip, Kevin, Steve, Marcus, Harry, Mark, Elaine and others in the Oxford gay and lesbian community.

We are discussing 'coming out', the decision lesbians and gays have to take as to whether they will publicly acknowledge their sexuality. Lis says, 'Gays and lesbians do not suddenly "come out" and that's it. We have to take decisions about when, how and to whom we "come out" every day, with every new friend we meet and in every fresh situation we encounter.'

Kevin, who helps run Oxford Friend, an organisation providing counselling services to gays and lesbians, tells me that the first problem for gay people is to acknowledge their sexuality to themselves. He gets three or four calls a week from married men and women who have denied their sexuality all their lives, had children in the hope that it would all 'go away' and then, often in later life, have to confront reality.

He says, 'If you could only somehow make people feel what it is like to be a member of a persecuted and misunderstood minority group; to imagine how they would feel faced with the prejudice lesbians and gays experience, it may improve their understanding. An upbringing of cosy heterosexual life, the knowledge that you are "normal", that you are accepted and approved by your parents and family, that you are condoned by the church and will not necessarily meet with aggression or ill feeling from your peers, cushions most heterosexual life. This is why so many gay men, or men with homosexual tendencies, marry and try to settle into a "safe" heterosexual lifestyle. The fear of pursuing their true sexual identity and the fear of discovery and all that might go with it, is too great. This leads to many problems in later life. We counsel many married men, some with families, who realise that the pressures of conforming to a "normal" lifestyle has led them to deceive their wives, children and, most of all, themselves. They are unhappy, full of guilt and desperately looking for a way to solve their problems. If only there was more tolerance towards being homosexual, these problems might not occur.'

Kevin continues, 'The anti-gay propaganda starts very early; youngsters coming to terms with their sexuality, when they have received no formal education about homosexuality, will only be told that homosexuality is "queer", not "normal", wrong and to be sneered and mocked at. Children use derogatory terms as insults, such as "queer", "poof" and "lezzie". This leads to feelings of isolation, self loathing and, in some cases, suicide. I cannot stress enough the need for formal sexual education which includes the basic facts about sexuality. I am not advocating any form of "promotion of homosexuality", just the facts presented with an understanding and caring attitude. I am appalled that the Tories are allowing parents to "opt out" their children from sex education and that teaching on homosexuality will not be included, at least not in a positive and understanding way. To my mind, good and caring sexual education is the basic fundamental way to change people's attitudes towards homosexuality. Fortunately, even without such formal education, most young people I meet seem naturally to have acquired a much more tolerant attitude than some of their elders. That, at least, gives me hope for the future.'

Marcus explains that, under the new education legislation, school governors are responsible for sex education. They naturally do not want to come under too much pressure from parents so there is, amongst school governors and teachers alike, a process of self-censorship which results, in many schools, in teaching about 'the plumbing', but ignoring the sexuality that lies behind it. Homosexuality is, in most cases, only mentioned where it is necessary in relation to HIV and Aids. This is highly dangerous since HIV and Aids is fast becoming a heterosexual as well as a homosexual disease and is a problem for all of us, not just the gay community. Even the medical school at Oxford has recently stopped including sexuality in its degree course for doctors. 'We will be in real trouble when even your doctor doesn't understand,' Kevin adds.

Mark, who runs a helpline in the centre, tells me that many gay youngsters discover their sexuality, just like heterosexuals, between the age of sixteen and twenty. But it is illegal to have homosexual intercourse under twenty-one (there is no lower age limit for lesbians). In practice, the police find this law difficult and enforce it in a very variable manner – which makes it impossible for young gays to know where they stand and sometimes leads to the law being applied in an uncertain and intimidatory manner.

He tells me that he often gets calls from parents wanting advice on how to handle their children's newly discovered sexuality. One mother, sensing that something was wrong, read her son's diary and discovered that he was gay. She rang to ask for help in dealing with this and for information about what his life would be like. But things are more often not so easy. Mark's own father initially refused to speak to him for more than six months after Mark had told him he was gay. And, on a recent evening when Mark was on the helpline switchboard, one youngster finally plucked up enough courage to speak to him on the sixteenth reverse charge phone call. It transpired that he was in a public phone box in only his underpants, having been thrown out of his home by his parents without any other clothes when he told them he was gay.

Elaine explains that discovering your sexuality in later life often leads to the break up of marriages. In these cases the courts almost always refuse to give the custody of the children to the homosexual partner, irrespective of the circumstances or wishes of the couple. She told me of one case in which she was recently involved, where the courts insisted on giving the custody of children from a marriage which was ended by the wife's discovery of her lesbian sexuality to the husband, even though he, she and the children had all agreed that they should stay with her. This ruling had eventually been overturned after a long and expensive court battle involving barristers. The children have grown up to be robustly and energetically heterosexual.

As have the children fostered by Judith and her partner. Judith, now in her fifties, has a face full of grace and compassion. She started fostering in 1974, when no one bothered to ask about foster parents' sexuality. She fostered her first child, Angela, who suffers from cerebral palsy and is now twenty one. Her second child, Elinor, was formally adopted as a baby and is now eighteen. Judith describes her as 'enthusiastically heterosexual'. Since then Judith and her partner have fostered or adopted fifty-two other children and will show you a full and delightful photograph album to prove it.

In the past she used to declare herself on the council forms as a single parent so as to make it easier for the council to ignore her sexuality. She says that the social workers who visited her certainly knew she was a lesbian, but chose to ignore it. But now things have been 'tightened up'. Few councils in Britain will accept gays and lesbians as suitable foster parents, even though this means that terribly handicapped children are left in institutions, when gay and lesbian couples are willing to provide them with a home and affection. Judith says, 'People do not yet know why some have good parenting skills, and others don't – but it certainly has nothing to do with their sexuality.' She tells me of a Hampshire lesbian couple, one of whom had three children by her previous marriage and the other worked in a paediatric ward. They had offered to provide respite care for very severely handicapped children but had been turned down by the county council as unsuitable.

A similar problem exists with personal and occupational insurance. Some insurance companies flatly refuse to insure gay people's lives. In other cases, gay people who assign their occupational insurance to their partner after their deaths can have their 'declaration of wish' overturned by the trustees or ultimately by the courts, if the deceased's family wish to mount a legal challenge to the dead person's wishes.

And most hospitals are little better. Elaine tells me of her ten-year relationship with a partner who had developed mental problems which, Elaine believes, arose from her denial of her own sexuality. Eventually Elaine persuaded her partner to go to her doctor who immediately referred her to an Oxford psychiatric hospital for treatment. The hospital told her that there was nothing they could do for her, gave her some pills and sent her home. When the problems persisted, Elaine became very worried and took her back. She visited the hospital with her partner eight times before the doctors agreed to an admission. The hospital doctors refused to speak to Elaine, who had lived with their patient for more than ten years, because she was 'not one of the family'. After a week in which the hospital again did nothing for her, Elaine's partner discharged herself. A little time later Elaine came home to find the garage door locked. When she broke it down she found her friend unconscious; she had tried to gas herself. She was rushed to another Oxford hospital, the John Radcliffe, where she took eight days to die. But the Radcliffe at least recognised Elaine's position and let her nurse her friend through the final days of her life. Elaine was allowed to stay permanently in her partner's room and no one objected when she put on a nightdress and climbed into the hospital bed so that she could hold her partner in her arms over her last three days of life.

In OXAIDS, they relate similar experiences. OXAIDS exists to provide help and support to people with Aids and HIV and to supply education and information to the public. The organisation, now jointly funded by Oxford city and county councils and the district and regional health authorities, was started in 1983 when a group of gay men in Oxford decided to act after reading about the effects of Aids in America and realising that no one in Britain was doing anything about it. Anna Eden, who works for OXAIDS, tells me that in 1983 there were a handful of people with Aids and HIV in the Oxford area. Today there are over 400.

Anna tells me that the progress of the disease is very unpredictable and varies from case to case. There is, apparently, no real watershed between HIV and Aids. In the US, Aids is diagnosed when the T4 blood cell count drops below 200. In Britain, the practice is to diagnose Aids according to the number and nature of symptoms identified in the patient. In some cases the onset of HIV can be accompanied by symptoms similar to glandular fever, after which there is an apparent complete recovery before, at some later date, other symptoms occur. In most cases, however, there are no symptoms when HIV is contracted – which is where the danger of the spread of infection lies. Nor is there any predictable progress for the disease. Some people diagnosed with HIV more than fifteen years ago have still not developed the full-blown disease. But, on average, around 50 per cent of those with HIV will develop Aids within ten years.

After many years of living well and in good health, people with HIV may begin to develop minor infections which indicate a depressed immune system. These might include diarrhoea, fungal infections, weight loss and other symptoms. Most of these infections can now be treated by conventional drugs and therapies. However, as the immune system deteriorates, other infections leading to illnesses such as tuberculosis and pneumonias can take place and cancers often begin to develop. Again, there are many treatments which can help control these illnesses or boost the immune system itself so that it can fight them off. One of the hardest aspects of living with HIV is not knowing how or when, or even if, illness may strike. Death is usually caused by the body being unable to tolerate the attacks of the diseases any longer.

Dave, who runs 'Body Positive', a self-help organisation for people with Aids and HIV, has the disease. He tells me that his T4 blood cell count is now down to 200 and that all those who were diagnosed with him are dead. He says that being diagnosed HIV positive forces you to focus on mortality and the real purposes of your life – this, as much as the disease, is what most people find so difficult to cope with.

OXAIDS and Body Positive provide a remarkable reservoir of compassion and assistance for people with this terrible disease. Those who assist come from all walks of life. People like Chris, who is a member of OXAIDS' 'buddy' group. Chris, probably in his early sixties, worked as a chartered surveyor for Oxford Colleges, and is married with three children. One day, about eight-

Above: 'Monktonhall, mothballed by British Coal, was opened up and the co-operative launched in 1988.'
Below: 'Big Andy does about four times the work I do.'

Above: 'A neat estate of modern bungalows, different, modern, individual.'
Below: 'Here are all the signs of human care and pride which seem so absent in the surrounding decay.'

Above: 'Paul, the local policeman, can now see growing trust between himself and the community.'
Right: 'Princes Avenue, once noble Victorian houses; today the houses are empty and boarded up. It is one of these that Godwin is converting to a home for ex-offenders.'

Above: 'The graffiti covers the
Gloucester Grove stairwells.'
Right: 'The squares between the blocks
of flats have become quagmires of mud,
bushes and blackness.'

Left: 'Weaving is delicate and skilled work which requires a high degree of concentration and dexterity.'
Below: 'The silk is spun off onto bobbins and dyed every colour imaginable.'

Above: 'Winston and I stop at Karl Seggree's roadside tea and snack bar.'
Below: 'A sense of desolation and hopelessness spreads out from the empty walkways and cracking concrete pillars.'

Top left: 'Del Puckey, the skipper.'
Above: 'The trawler bucks and pitches its way onto the sea.'
Below: 'The sea suddenly breaks into a surge of froth as the net mouth comes to the surface.'

Above: 'We must be careful not to drop the round bales sideways onto the hill.'
Below: 'Afterwards, dinner. With the silage crew, John's brother and others, we are now eight around the table.'

een months ago, he decided that he wanted to help people with Aids – 'There but for the grace of God go I.' After initial training, he has now been accepted as a member of the 'buddy' group, whose job is to befriend lonely and often shunned people suffering from Aids and ensure that they do not die alone. Chris's first buddy died before he could establish a relationship with him. He is at present providing friendship and support to a man rejected by his family and shunned by his friends who is so paralysed by his disease, frightened about his forthcoming death and angry with the world that Chris admits that his obviously immense reserves of patience are tested to the full in communicating with his dying buddy.

Many people, however, have more control over their lives and deaths than is commonly thought. Mary, an OXAID worker, describes what happened to her friend Tom, who was thirty-five years old. Tom died quite peacefully but had suffered badly in the year before. He was, nevertheless, able to maintain his job up to the last month of his life through regular blood transfusions. Eventually these had to get more and more frequent until the hospital said that they could help no longer. Tom had carefully planned his own funeral. His brother rang from America to say that he would be coming over to see him on the following Friday. Tom replied, 'No, come sooner.' The brother answered, 'How about Wednesday?' Tom said that would do. Tom died the following Thursday.

I left Oxford with my prejudices severely unseated and very moved by the dignity and compassion of the people I had met and those who help them.

Chapter 20

'We are going to win and the industrial West is going to lose. There is nothing you can do about it because the reasons for your failure are in yourself. Your bosses are doing the thinking, while the workers wield the screwdriver: you are convinced deep down that this is the right way to run a business.'

21–22 June 1993

To Derby to visit the Toyota car factory and Johnson Control Automotive (JCA) factory in Burton.

◆

They look for all the world like four surgeons peering into a body, discussing amongst themselves what needs to be done and then, quietly and purposefully going about their work. I watch as one turns, puts down one implement and carefully selects another, moves forward, head down squinting into the body cavity; the head tilts slightly as if to get a better look and then moves forward delicately and precisely and puts a pair of calipers onto the anatomy – a brief hiss, a shower of sparks and it moves on. Elsewhere its colleagues are quietly going about their work on different parts of the body, all nodding and moving and hissing as though in an elegant and pre-arranged dance.

What they are building in the pit six or eight feet below me is a car. There are three car bodies being methodically put together by three teams of four robots. There are no humans down there. Past me, like attendant nurses, glide other wheeled robots, silent apart from their warning beep, carrying batches of sheet metal to the huge presses which gravely accept them, shape them and hand them on to the team of body builders in the pit.

Around me in this press shop, thirteen metres high and 375 metres long, it is as clean as an operating theatre and almost as well lit. What comes in here as sheet metal leaves the final production line in an adjacent building twenty-five hours later as a Toyota Carina E car. In this shop, assembling 200 car bodies a day, there are 160 robots and fewer than 200 people. The humans are so widely dispersed in this huge cavern that it is often possible to look round and see no one – just their silent and purposeful assistants obediently going about their work. As we walk round, a fully assembled car body passes over our heads and into the next-door paint shop every two minutes.

I ask Bryan Jackson, a Director of Toyota who is showing me around and who has spent a life time in the car industry, how many people would have worked in such a press and weld shop ten years ago. 'A very great deal more,' is his laconic reply.

Toyota, now among the top three of the world's leading car manufacturers by volume, invested £700 million in this Derby car manufacturing factory and a further £140 million in an engine manufacturing plant in North Wales to feed it. Work on this site began in 1990 and the first car rolled off the production line in December 1992.

I have come here not to marvel at automation, but to learn about the new working practices, management style and production techniques which many believe Britain will have to adopt if we are going to re-build our manufacturing industries again. I am being shown around by Bryan Jackson and the Managing Director of Toyota in Derby, Yukihisa Hirano.

The new factory lies just outside Derby. Its visual impact on the countryside around is discreetly diminished by careful landscaping. Toyota make a selling point of their environmental sensitivity. They tell me that they use only water-based paints on their cars and spend a great deal of money and effort on reducing emissions to the atmosphere from this plant.

Inside, there is the same care about cleanliness and order. There is none of the clutter and clatter and dirt of engineering production as I have known it. The layout of the production lines is deceptively simple, the floors are greaseless and spotlessly clean, the workers (Toyota call their employees 'members') neatly turned out. Kerry Oakes, Bryan Jackson's secretary, who picked me up from Derby station, told me that the company make available their own Toyota work-wear for members who want to use it. There is no compulsion to wear it but most do.

Order and routine are a vital part of the production process. Each job is divided up into 'standard work processes'. Anyone can suggest a change to a standard work process. But while a work process is in force, everyone is expected to follow it precisely, even to the exact position in which, for instance, a component is placed on a pallet. This is to enable them to reduce the number of variables that have to be considered when a snag or defect occurs. Everyone is dedicated – almost fanatical – about discovering defects and solving problems. When, recently, they increased the speed of the production line from 150 to 200 cars a day, what everyone was pleased about was not the increased production, but the number of defects and problems which came to light and were solved.

Mr Hirano tells me, as we walk round, that all Toyota staff are organised in teams. Each team or cell is four or five strong and fully responsible for everything it does. Safety, for instance, is of primary importance. Every member is responsible for their own safety and that of their team. Stopping the production line is extremely expensive. But any member at any level is entitled to do it if they think the quality of the product has been adversely affected.

Quality is the first duty of every worker. The target is 100 per cent defect-free production, both from Toyota and from their suppliers. Mr Hirano says, 'It is the duty of every member to assure quality and identify defects, whether they are responsible for them or not. It doesn't matter who is responsible for a defect, it is Toyota and their reputation with the customer which suffers – so it is the responsibility of all of us to put it right.'

Bryan Jackson tells me that achieving quality means 'everyone accepting the fact that they have a positive role to play'. He says, 'When we train our members, we train them to think about everything they do and why they do it. We want members who will question and suggest and improve. The traditional British attitude is that managers use their brains, workers use their hands. I do not accept that. Here we expect every member, whether management or shop-floor, to use both their brain and their hands.' As I watch, I notice that there is no apparent vertical management hierarchy on the shop floor. Everyone seems to communicate laterally, networking with their colleagues, rather than taking orders from above.

On the way round I suggest to Simon Mansfield, an assembly-line team leader, that the order, routine and emphasis on team work is de-humanising. He tells me that, on the contrary, he gets real satisfaction from this style of working. 'There is nothing more satisfying than working as a team. We're not individuals here – we are a team. But we can each put in our own ideas and we can each discuss these and improve the system and the quality as we go along. We call it "Kaizenning the process" – the word comes from the Japanese word "Kaizen", which means continuous improvement – and its the secret of quality.'

Behind him hangs a notice which reads 'Good thinking equals good products'.

Bryan tells me that, after recruiting their workforce, they sent many to Japan for training at Toyota's main factory. There they picked up and returned with many practices which are used in Japan, but which the company did not think it essential to bring to Britain. One was the use of Japanese words, like 'Kaizen'. These words had, nevertheless, become standard currency among the UK workforce. Similarly, many had brought back the Japanese practice of doing exercises before work. This, too, is not compulsory, but a large proportion of the Derby work-force choose to come to work early in order to take part in the pre-work exercise sessions. This has caused some suspicion and amusement amongst the wider population of Derby. But Kerry Oakes, on our way from the station, told me that she did not find it at all odd. 'If you are going to start a day's work in which everything you do has to be the highest quality, you should make sure your body's fit for it.'

Work begins each morning at 7.40 a.m. for those who wish to do exercises. Then each team meets for five or ten minutes to discuss quality problems and the lessons learnt from the previous day. This time is not paid. At 8 a.m. sharp, a buzzer sounds and the production lines start. At 10 a.m., the line halts for fifteen minutes. Five minutes of this are spent in a team meeting and ten on a break.

As we make our way to one of Toyota's canteens (there are two canteens which are used by everyone, whatever their status), Bryan tells me that British firms have tried to copy these techniques by 'cherry picking' what they consider the best practices. 'If you want to do it properly, you have to have the whole lot, including adapting the philosophy that's behind it.' Bryan continues, 'Our secret is that we value our workforce. We value our members. We nurture them, we train, we provide them with good terms and conditions and we make sure that they understand and blossom in our culture. Of the 1,200 people who work here, we believe that everyone's job is important and everyone recognises the importance of everyone else's. The key principle of our style of management is "mutual trust and respect". This means that when we make decisions we do not do so on a snap basis, we consult our workforce and make sure that we have the support of the consensus. It sometimes means that decisions take longer, but it nearly always means that they last longer, too. Lastly, we always take the long view. British industry has suffered probably more because of short-term thinking than for any other reason.'

Mr Hirano makes the same point in another way. 'It took us two and a half years to build this factory. But it will take us ten years to train the workforce and smooth out the production snags sufficiently to bring it up to its full production level.'

He goes on to describe the difference between British workers and those in Japan. 'Over the weekend, I had a problem with the alarm system in my house. The police came round and said I should call British Telecom. The BT engineer came round and said it wasn't his responsibility, I must call the alarm company. The alarm company man came round and blamed it on a component supplier. What we are trying to create in Toyota is members who will say "You are our customer so we will see it is fixed for you." '

Over lunch Bryan Jackson tells me about the factory's recruitment policy. The company had 20,000 applications for the 1,200 new jobs in Derby. What they looked for was people who were courageous, self motivated and showed a capacity to think for themselves. What he wants from the education system is a broad education which would provide the basis for learning and adapting in the future, not just narrow specialist qualifications. But that does mean a good grounding in the basics of language and mathematics.

After lunch I leave Mr Hirano and Bryan Jackson and choose a nearby table, which I join. This turns out to be staff from the factory's 'human resources' division – what most firms would call 'personnel'. Philip Young and Clive Bridge describe how they recruited their members. 'Initially we set up a profile of the kind of people we want. We then developed a detailed selection system for every position, including those on the shop floor. Every applicant has to go through at least three stages to get the job. These include aptitude tests, a half-day simulation, a personnel interview and an extensive medical. We spend more time and care selecting a shop-floor member than most companies do choosing middle or even senior management. It's often tough to get in here, but once you're in you are really valued.'

I leave this group and join a production team lunching at a nearby table. They were made up of people who had previously worked in a wide variety of jobs, including the coal, steel and retail industries. I tell them I am sceptical about all this order and self-discipline. But they seemed genuinely enthusiastic about their jobs and the work style. Some, notably those from the steel and mining industries, said that in their previous jobs they did not feel valued; no one wanted to know what they thought. Here anyone could stop the line, or make a suggestion or change things. You were expected to think, and what you thought mattered. One, Peter Vince, says, 'They tell you everything that's going on – it makes you feel part of the operation. If all the industries in Britain could work like this, we'd be top of the league. Do you know, Toyota's dealers in Europe are already saying they prefer our cars to the Japanese made ones. It's bloody brilliant.'

Ray Lambert, who recently had a football injury, comments on the fact that he was not hassled to return to work. He was told to make sure he really got better first. Craig Woodhead praises the private health scheme to which every worker is entitled. His wife had to have an operation which would have meant a wait of up to eighteen months on the NHS. But, under the company scheme, she was taken in straight away.

Before I leave, Mr Hirano tells me of the importance they attach to quality in their component and equipment suppliers. 'We spent nearly two years before we started up checking and helping our component suppliers to achieve the quality Toyota requires. Sometimes we even took them to Japan to give them the chance to see suppliers operating there. It was difficult to get them to understand our "just in time" production system which requires our components to be exactly where we want them, exactly when they are needed. And it was even more difficult to get some of them to realise that we really did want 100 per cent defect-free goods. Some firms who wanted our business used to take great pride in the fact that they were reducing their defects. I had patiently to explain to them that it wasn't good enough unless they were 100 per cent free of defects.'

I had arranged to take a look at one of Toyota's suppliers and Kerry drives me to Johnson Control Automotive's (JCA) factory in Burton-upon-Trent. This, too is a new factory, built by JCA specifically to enable them to win the Toyota supply contract. They make the seats for the Carina E.

JCA in Burton is run by Eammon Kearney, who is thirty-six, left school with average, but not outstanding, qualifications, part trained as an accountant and describes himself as a 'late developer'. He is an impressive and effective manager who follows the same management style as Toyota. He tells me that JCA's motto is 'exceeding the customer's expectations' and this is done in four ways: price, service, quality and innovation.

He, too, looked for workers who are honest, courageous and not afraid to express their views. Once selected, again after a rigorous and extended selection procedure, it is rare to have to get rid of a member of the JCA team. Eammon tells me, 'When we take someone on we equip them with the techniques to enable them to improve their own quality and manage their own work. We look particularly for the long-term unemployed, because we want to mould unmoulded material. Some say this is brain-washing. But if allowing people to think and act for themselves is brain washing, then give me more of it. The secret of our success lies in valuing and respecting our work force – recognising that each of them has an important job and a contribution to make – understanding that you can only make quality goods if you have a quality work force.'

Steve Spratt, JCA's Operations Manager, picks up the point. 'Not long ago I gathered sixteen people together to tell them what the firm was doing and what we should do next. I suddenly realised that in my audience there was a total of 260 years of experience in thirty-two different jobs. Who was I to be telling them what to do? It ought to be my job, as the leader, to draw out of them their experience and this would help make the job we do better for all of us. Many of the people who work with me run football teams, are guide leaders, chair local organisations or just run good and effective families when they are not at work. These are intelligent people with a lot to offer. Why should we treat them like morons, just because they are in the work place?'

I spend the afternoon working with the JCA 'members' on their production line. Karen Charlesworth tells me that what she likes about the firm is that you can just walk into anyone's office and tell them what you think and your opinion is valued. 'There aren't any barriers here. If anything goes wrong it's up to every-one to put it right,' she says.

Dave Bird, in his previous job a steel worker and a shop steward for the T&GWU, says that he gets real satisfaction out of this job, which he never did from his previous one. I am concerned that there isn't any union in the factory. He says, 'Why do we need one? I would rather tell the boss what I think directly than put it through the mouth of a union official.'

Fred Williams, black with luxuriant dreadlocks, and one of the team leaders, tells me that the thing he enjoys is the fact that there is no 'them and us'. He adds, 'We used to be the best engineers in the world and we can be again, if only people will recognise that you have to value people, not use them.'

In the late afternoon Eammon tells me about 'just in time' production. The aim is to cut down stocks and reduce the working capital tied up in holding large amounts of raw material and finished goods. Just as JCA was required to produce just in time for Toyota, so JCA require its producers to supply the components they need to build their seats just in time to JCA. This means that every producer has to have a very close and sensitive relationship with their customer. 'We work hand in glove with Toyota and our suppliers have to work hand in glove with us. That's the way "just in time" production works,' Eammon explains.

If JCA failed to supply a single component on time to Toyota, the whole production line would stop, incurring huge costs. There therefore has to be absolute trust between customer and supplier. If JCA hits problems, then it is not unusual for Toyota to send a team of engineers down to help them solve them. By the same token, Toyota recognises JCA as experts in seat manufacture and would accept suggestions from them about changes in work practices and even in design.

I can see how close the relationship is when I join in on the JCA production line. At the end of the line is a small printer which tells JCA what they must build, individual seat by individual seat. As each Toyota car goes from the press shop into the paint shop at the factory fifteen miles away, a message goes automatically to the start of the JCA production line telling them exactly what seat to build for that car. They then build the seat and deliver it to the Toyota production line to meet its designated car as it emerges into the assembly shop precisely six hours later.

I am standing at the start of the JCA line at 13.50 exactly when the next docket is printed. It calls for a seat set for a Carina XL, with vertical height adjustment, grey, for a left-hand drive car. Steve Spratt, who manages JCA production, tells me that this individual car was probably ordered from one of Toyota's European dealers yesterday.

'It won't stop there,' he continues. 'In America you can now order a car to your precise specifications on Monday and take delivery of it the following Friday. In future you won't order cars from showroom stock, you will have them made individually to your choice at the factory. British industry has to understand that it can only survive if it can match world standards – that means that we have to do whatever others can do, only better.'

Eammon describes 'just in time' production as 'like a drug'. 'You are always living on the edge of your chair, everyone has to be pulling their weight – everyone has to be thinking all the time – everyone has to realise that, if something goes wrong it's not "your" problem, or "his" problem, its our problem and we'd all better solve it.'

I left Derby the following day thinking that was a good motto for a firm – an even better one for a country.

———————

Chapter 21

'There are three things in life which are important – your family, your friends and your farming.'

27–29 June 1993

To the Wye valley to spend two days and nights with John Lloyd and his family on their farm above Hay-on-Wye.

♦

If you are tired of life, drive into the marches of Wales on the road from Talgarth to Clyro on a sunny day and try to believe that there is not a God and happiness.

Today started off as one of those days when everything seems to go wrong. I was not in the best of moods when I left Somerset and drove over the Severn and into Wales. And my frustration was not eased by the fact that the roads are full of tourists and summer traffic. But the traffic thins by the time I get to Crickhowell and start the long ascent over the mountains to Talgarth and the Wye valley. It is a day of sunny patches and thin low cloud resting on the mountains. As I come over the top of the mountain, there, suddenly, is the Wye valley and the border marches of Wales laid out before me in the sunlight.

In front are the rolling grass ridges, darkening with heather towards Wales. To the north a patchwork quilt of fields, with winter barley ripening to a pale yellow and seeming to reflect the sun. In the middle of the valley, the Wye flowing blue, slow and clear, gathering as it goes fast brown streams which roll, energetic and vibrant, over rocks, down the valleys and through stands of conifer to meet it. There are white houses and dark, slate-coloured farmsteads and great woods of stout trees growing blue in the distance and, here and there, the red earth of newly ploughed fields. And to my right, over Hay-on-Wye, the Black

Mountains and Hay Bluff stand green, clear and clean above the wooded valleys. However miserable you are, you cannot remain so at such a sight.

In half an hour I am through Clyro and have climbed the steep ridge to John Lloyd's farm high on the hill above the Wye valley. There are wild roses at the farm gate and in front of me, at the end of 200 yards of farm track, is John's farm, Cefn-y-Blaen, which means in Welsh 'the house with the front at the back of the hill'.

The farmhouse itself lies, sturdy and grey, with its out buildings gathered about it, at the head of a bowl and just under the crest of the hill. Around it: a garden which bears all the marks of careful tending, a beautifully manicured lawn, neat grey stone walls and flower beds with rockery plants glowing with the colours of June. Behind is a conifer wood protecting it from the north wind and in front fields leading down to a wooded stream valley, beyond which roll the dappled hills west into Wales.

As I drive up, two men are bending over a tractor. One shouts towards the house 'Mother, our guest has arrived.' I am introduced to John Lloyd and his family.

John himself is everyone's idea of what a Welsh farmer should be: round, strong, of medium height, with a wonderfully brown, lined walnut face, light blue eyes and pronounced laughter lines around which there seems permanently to be hovering some joke or chuckle. He has a stature which speaks of a life walking on these hills, hard work, good beer and a laugh which sounds like water gurgling over stones. He looks what he is; a man deeply happy with his lot in life. Over the next two days that I work with him, I will never hear him once complain, or criticise, or say a harsh word about anyone around him.

His wife Joan is trim, homely and soft spoken. Like the rest of her family, she has no side and shows absolutely no embarrassment or difficulty in dealing with this stranger who has suddenly been thrust into their midst.

The young man who acknowledged my arrival from the bowels of his tractor turns out to be Andrew, John's son, six foot one, with a square powerful frame, a shock of fair hair and one of those faces which instinctively engenders trust. Andrew has recently taken over Cefn-y-Blaen with his new wife, red-haired

Meryl, who is the daughter of a farmer and now works in a local bank.

Over lunch and afterwards John, who is hardly ever seen without a pipe in his mouth, but seems to consume more matches than tobacco, tells me the story of Cefn-y-Blaen. He and Joan moved here from John's family farm over the hill when they were first married more than thirty years ago. The house and the land were then totally derelict. Many of the fields which now surround the farmhouse like a green mantle were strewn with stone and covered in bracken, gorse and wood. He and Joan cleared them all single handedly, with only the aid of an old tractor.

The farm house had only one downstairs room which they used in the early years to shelter the weaker ewes and lambs, John carrying them up to the house one by one on his back with the newly born lambs stuffed in his pockets. Over the years they had built the garden, added to the house to bring it up to its present comfortable size, constructed more outhouses and barns and purchased more land to make this an established and sizeable farm.

John now has 254 acres of his own, rents a further 150 acres and has recently acquired another farmhouse and a further thirty-four acres in a sale. On this he keeps 1,600 breeding ewes, 2,000 lambs and eighty suckler cows and their calves. It has been hard work. John and Joan have had only one proper long holiday in their thirty years of marriage. 'If you go farming, you can forget the villa in France,' he says. 'This is a seven day a week, work-as-long-as-there's-work-to-do job. I reckon that, over a year, I must work for about 60 pence an hour. But I love it and I would not do anything else. There are three things in life which matter: your family, your friends and your farming. The important thing is to get them in the right order. Can't say I've always managed that – probably put farming first too much,' he adds, shooting a look at his wife.

John describes his farming year to me. In January, they are busy with early lambing. February is spent feeding ewes which are coming up to the main lambing in March and April, one of their busiest times of the year. The sheep are let out in April. In May they shut off some of the fields to allow time for the grass to grow for silage. May is also busy with the task of castrating, docking and pitching (marking) lambs. Shearing is done in June, which also sees the start of silage and hay-making and the 'tupping' of ewes who will produce next year's early January lambs. July and August are marketing months. During August they cut thistles and re-seed the fields. The main crop of ewes are taken to the rams for tupping in September and this goes on into October. November is usually John's lightest month, taken up with markets and buying replacement stock and occasionally a couple of days' snatched holiday in Tenby. December sees the start of winter feeding of the stock and the weaning of calves.

John and Joan are now in their early fifties, when most people who have achieved as much as they have would sit back and enjoy it. Instead, having handed over Cefn-y-Blaen, house, land and all, to Andrew and Meryl, John's new challenge is to renovate the stout but rather tumbledown sixteenth-century Radnorshire farmhouse and land he and Joan have bought, at the bottom of the hill.

It soon transpires that John is not just a farmer – he is also a trader, contractor, small businessman and entrepreneur. His second love after farming is making a deal and his second joy, when he's not on his land, is going to market. Apart from farming his own land, he does contract work for friends and neighbours, buys, bales and sells straw when the market is right, markets livestock for farmers who don't like marketing, and is prepared to turn his hand to any deal in which there is the joy of trading and a bit of profit to be made. He says, 'There is a strong tradition amongst farmers in this area that we all help each other – and we do. But when you go to market, then it's each one for himself. The aim is to get a little more than your neighbour for your beasts and if you do, even if it's only a few pence, then you feel you've won the race.'

After lunch, there is a tractor handbrake to be mended. John and Andrew weld a home-made device to make the brake easier and safer to operate on these steep-sided fields. This evening, the contractor who cuts the grass for silage comes and they will start one of the busiest periods of the year. So the tractors must be in full working order.

Afterwards we go down to visit one of John's neighbours, Margi

James at Crossfoot farm. Margi's husband is an estate agent. But farming is her passion and Crossfoot is her love. As we arrive there is a clatter of ducks and geese and dogs and cats. John rents some of her land and does much of her contract work – we will return tomorrow to bale some hay which has been cut and left to dry on a lower field. At the end of the year, the pair of them sit down with a bottle of whisky, add up who has done what for whom and then settle the difference in a single session.

There is obviously a good deal of fun between them as well as trust. John tells me that, one April Fool's Day, he arrived at Crossfoot to collect some of his sheep that had been left there, to find them all painted red, white and blue. He retaliated a little later by tying the dead stiff body of a fox in an upright position on Margaret's tractor seat. She came out, bleary eyed in the half light of morning, and jumped up on the tractor to be greeted by this ghoulish sight. The joke worked: she screamed and ran off.

We cross back over the hill to visit another neighbour, John Bally, who has 210 acres in the valley bottom below Cefn-y-Blaen, in which he farms deer. John Bally, master of the local hounds, a member of the British gliding team, a one-time professional yachtsman and a keen mountaineer, is also an enthusiastic conservationist and passionate countryman. He takes me round his farm, on which he has forty stags, 120 deer calves and the same number of hinds, as well as 650 breeding ewes, producing 900 lambs. He tells me, with some venom, of the destructive habits of magpies which kill large numbers of young birds on the farm. He shows me the areas of his farm where he is trying to use land management to create a haven for wild flowers and orchids. John is extremely critical of the present conservation legislation which he says will not work in areas like this, unless it is dramatically revised.

'What we have to realise,' he says, 'is that nature has to be managed and conservation, if we want it, has to be paid for. In stock-rearing country like this, woodlands and coverts are dying a slow death. If stock are fenced out of woodland, then the farmer loses his Hill Live Stock Compensation Allowance of £60 per hectare for the ground which is fenced off. No farmer round here can afford to lose that kind of money. If the woodland areas are not fenced off then every new shoot is eaten and the woods die. There is a new scheme for Environmentally Sensitive Areas which offers £70 compensation per hectare for fenced woodland. But round here, we use woods to shelter our animals in hard weather and if we are to fence them off then extra shelter has to be built for the stock, which costs much more than the compensation which is offered. I have a twenty-acre wood which gives shelter to 300 sheep in winter. Putting up a building to provide alternative shelter would cost £20,000. How can the scheme work?

'Meanwhile, the compensation schemes encourage farmers to put more and more land down to grass. In these hills that means steep fields with sixty-degree slopes are ploughed and seeded to grass, at great risk to life. You would not believe it possible. Presumably, when seen on paper, the bureaucrats think the fields are flat! Top soil is washed off and lost for ever, a poor swarth eventually gets established. The farmer cannot be blamed. Grass is meat and meat is money. Tragically the cost is loss of habitat and woodlands. Meanwhile the incentives exist to plant in arable country, whilst the hills become a grass desert.'

By 6 p.m. we are back at Cefn-y-Blaen, where Joan has dinner ready for us. The silage contractor has arrived and after dinner the silage making begins and continues until the light goes. I feel particularly useless at such a busy time, not being able to drive a tractor and having to stand and watch without being able to help. It will take six or seven days' hard continuous work to cut all John's fields and fill the silage clamp. The grass must be dry, or too much effluent will be produced which poisons the water table and the local rivers. They often work on beyond midnight and have been known to work twenty-four or more hours at a stretch if the weather looks likely to change. But tonight the weather is settled and fair and John wants to take me to his local.

Before darkness falls, John takes me round the farm, checking his livestock. He especially wants to look at some cows which are coming close to calving and to check the newly born calves to ensure they are feeding properly on their mother's milk. We go round the northern borders of the farm and look down on the farmhouse where John grew up and where his brother now farms. He tells me how, as a boy, he walked every day from this house the four and a half miles to school and back over the fields he now owns and farms. The sky is now clearing and we have a magnificent view of the Wye valley and the Welsh hills. Immediately below us in the valley bottom is Rhosgoch bog, where John tells me he used to shoot snipe and woodcock. It is now, rightly he says, a nature reserve which is only disturbed a few times a year when it is drawn for foxes.

This is an old land with a sense of magic about it, especially in this evening light. As we walk round I quietly reflect that, whatever I may achieve in politics, I shall never be able to match the sense of personal achievement which this man and his wife will have, having been brought up on this land, building a successful farm from it and then being able to hand it over to their son.

The evening is spent at the Castlefield Inn on the other side of Hay-on-Wye with local farmers and their wives. The talk is of farming and livestock and silage and politics and it is much enlivened by the Castlefield Inn's landlord who is famous for being blunt to the point of rudeness with his customers, whoever they are. At one stage I ask them whether they are Welsh or English? They say that in Hereford, they are referred to as Welsh and in Builth Wells they are treated as English, but they consider themselves to be people of the Marches. After four pints of beer, topped off with a whisky, I fall into bed at Cefn-y-Blaen at 1 a.m., dreading the hangover I shall have next day.

By the time I am up at 7a.m., John has already come up from the lower farm, worked an hour and a half and cut two fields of grass for the silage contractor. As I help him mend one of his grass cutters I hear on the tractor radio that the Americans have bombed Baghdad. It seems curiously impossible on this bright early June morning in the Wye valley.

After a farmhouse breakfast I am off to visit two more local farms: Bill Davies, who farms a thousand acres in the valley bottom where the land is excellent and grows good arable crops, and Cherry Phillips, who single handedly farms land on the broad open valley above Hay on Wye. Bill tells me that, in his father's time, they farmed 500 acres here and employed seven men. Now he farms 1,000 acres and employs two. 'And now,' he says, 'because we have been too successful, too efficient, we have to start producing less. I can see why we have to do it, but it seems curious, when we have always been encouraged by governments to try to produce more. Now they want us to take some of our land out of production. I find it immoral to take land that has been cleared, tended and cared for by my ancestors in this valley and let it go back to what it was. Under the new regulations, farmers will be paid to let as much as a fifth of their land go wild permanently. The public aren't going to like that when the see the countryside change. And they are going to understand even less, when they hear that farmers are getting paid to let their land go derelict and unsightly. Many farmers think this "set aside" scheme is quite wrong. If they want us to produce less from the land, a better way to achieve it would be to limit the nitrogen we are able to apply. Many farmers are already putting far too much nitrogen on their land and some are putting on so much on they are ruining the ground. If they put a tax on nitrogen, they would force farmers back to older, safer methods of husbandry, like crop rotation. This would keep the land in production, rather than letting it go back to wilderness, which I and many others think is offensive to everything we stand for.'

We find Cherry Phillips baling in the middle of a field in the bright June sunshine and she takes me to see the herd of Herefords which she, her parents and grandparents have reared here since they took over the farm in 1923. Cherry is now one of the last farmers to keep a large herd of Herefords round here. Afterwards we go to her magnificent farm house, originally built by the monks of the nearby Priory in the twelfth century. Outside there are grey stone barns, massive and solid, surrounding the yard. Inside the house is huge, cool, oak beamed with high ceilings, deep cellars and a powerful sense of being lived in century after century by people who drew their strength from the ground and gave it back into their houses and possessions.

It is now a glorious, cloudless blue and perfect day. As we drive out of the ancient court yard, Cherry tells me that she thinks that this land has been farmed in almost exactly the same way since her parents came here, seventy years ago. Suddenly I recall that my father, just before he died, used to talk a lot about his boyhood when, unable to return to his parents in India, he had spent school holidays with an uncle who was a parson near Hay on Wye and how he loved the country here and first became infected with his passion for country sports in the woods and streams of this valley. For a moment I have a vivid picture of him as fourteen-year-old walking these hedgerows with a gun or rod in his hand on a bright summer's day such as this.

After lunch back at Cefn-y-Blaen, I help John round bale the hay in Margi James's fields at Crossfoot. The field is very steep and directly above the main road to Hereford. John tells me that we must be careful not to drop the round bales sideways on to the hill or they will roll down and drop the 200 feet or so onto the road below. He lets me try. The second bale I do seems to have a life of its own. It turns and, in a second, is thundering off, rolling in a gathering cloud of dust towards the hill edge and the road below. John and I watch helplessly as the thought flashes through my mind of newspaper headlines about innocent tourists being killed in their car by the leader of the Liberal Democrats trying his hand at farming. But fortunately the final fence above the road holds the bale. I breathe a sigh of relief and hand the tractor back to John, who laughs a great deal and anticipates the stories he will be able to tell at my expense in the pub in future.

There is worse to come when we return to Cefn-y-Blaen; fed up with not being able to do anything useful, I persuade Andrew to show me how to use a tractor to roll the silage pit. I almost immediately succeed in nearly tipping the great beast over and have to be rescued by a mirthful Andrew. But he is patient and I soon get the hang of it. Afterwards, dinner. With the silage crew, John's brother who has come to help, and various others, we are now eight around the farmhouse table and Joan and Meryl hover round the outside to make sure everyone's plates are full.

The talk is of farm subsidy. That morning, John and I had heard a report on the tractor radio of figures issued today showing that every family of four in Europe now pays £1000 per year in extra food prices, to give every farmer a subsidy of £10,000 a year. John sucked his teeth when he heard the report and said that the public simply would not tolerate such a thing for long. I asked him what would happen if the subsidies were withdrawn.

He answered, 'Oh, in that case, we'd be beat, boy – we'd be beat.'

What now comes to light, however, is that the subsidy is often not ultimately of benefit to the farmer as much as it is to the supermarket. John tells me of a lone campaign he and a neighbour James Gibson Watt have fought to get fair prices for farmers from the supermarkets.

In November 1991, John and James suddenly realised that a lamb of, say seventeen kilos dead weight, for which they were getting £24, was being sold in the supermarket for £90. The two of them started to trace the progress of the lamb carcass to see if they could discover how the price increase was justified. They went to the local abattoir and found that they were paid no more than fractions of a pence per kilo for killing the beast – most abattoirs kill for the price of the lamb skin. One large abattoir, with a near monopoly of lamb purchases in this part of the country, had recently expanded their facilities and now bought, packed and despatched meat for all five big supermarkets. They bought in lambs from the farmer at one end and sent them out at the other, packaged, labelled and priced for the supermarket, at a value more than four times what the farmer received. Nor was the problem confined to meat. A friend of John's sold his cauliflowers at 2 or 3 pence each, to find them being resold less than twenty-four hours later in a supermarket chain for 70 pence.

Over the months, John and James put together powerful evidence of collusion in some local markets of the unhealthy monopoly buying power of the five major supermarkets and of the massive profits being made by them at the farmer's expense. Right throughout the recession, while farmers were being especially hard hit, the profits of the big supermarket chains remained buoyant – the previous year Tesco had made more profit than Barclays bank.

John and James went to see the National Farmers' Union in London about it but were told 'Don't hit your best customer – drop it.' They went to see the Office of Fair Trading who said they were very interested, promised action, but then mysteriously did nothing. They eventually got a BBC farming programme interested. The BBC duly did a programme on the subject. Afterwards John and James suddenly found themselves blacked at some of the local markets.

John says, 'It takes a farmer a full year to raise a lamb, but the people who make the profit are the supermarkets – they make 300 per cent in a couple of days. But of course, it's not the farmer who pays for this, it's the public. If we got fair farm-gate prices for our produce, then we wouldn't need subsidies to survive. The situation is not so bad now. There is still a 300–400 per cent markup of prices by the supermarkets. But now, thanks to the single European market, we are able to sell overseas to the Continent. So the supermarkets' monopoly on the meat market has been broken. But for more perishable goods like vegetables, which cannot be sold abroad, the situation is still just as bad.'

Afterwards John and I go down into the valley in the gathering summer dusk to bale some hay on a lower meadow. It is a large field and takes longer than we thought. As I stand and watch, James Gibson-Watt calls by and invites me back to his neighbouring farm house for a beer and a chat.

I leave him at around ten and return through the dusk to John, who is still baling in the field where I left him. As I walk through James Gibson-Watt's farmyard and across the fields, the smell of the rising dew and roses mingles with the musty scent of sheep and cattle settling down for the night. The velvet colours of dusk have given way to darkness, save for a thin rim of failing light on the high ridge in front of me, against which the trees and woods of the crest are sharply etched. Below on the dark mountain, little pricks of light from white farm house windows dot the hillside. Around me, the sounds of night are only interrupted by the gentle grumble of John's tractor, headlights glowing, still busy in the field below.

On such a night as this it is not difficult to see why John Lloyd and his ancestors have spent long lives putting such pride and beauty into this land.

Chapter 22

'We have a society which values money and uses people, when what we need is a society which uses money and values people.'

28–29 June 1993

To Littlehampton in Sussex where I spend the day with the staff of Westcourt surgery and the night with Dr John Latham and his family.

◆

Job Langton was a desert rat during World War Two. He sits on the sofa, his eyes bright, as we discuss military affairs and his experiences in the Western desert. He does not look like a man who is a week from death. Maureen Dobbelaar, Job's district nurse, tells me later that this is the effect of the steroids. Job's wife Sheila sits beside him. It was Sheila who opened the door to us tearfully – 'Job's not been so well today' – when we arrived. It is Sheila who has been with him throughout his long fight with stomach cancer. It was Sheila who took him to the Marsden Hospital for his regular chemotherapy. It was Sheila who the hospital told when they discovered that Job's cancer had moved to the liver and that there was nothing more they could do. It was Sheila who had to tell Job he had a month to live, who had to cope with his depression and who now tends and cares for him as he waits for death.

And it is Sheila who will soon confide to me, while Job is upstairs being given treatment by Maureen, that she wants him to die 'wherever it suits him' – which at present, Job says, is at home with her. But Sheila, full of courage, dignity and determination, is worried that she may not have the strength to help him through the last few days.

Sheila currently receives the standard allowance of £44.90 per week for those caring for loved ones who are expected to die within the next six months. If Job has to go into a hospital at the end, it will cost the state £250 per day – slightly less if he dies in a hospice. Whether Sheila will be able to cope will depend on what support Maureen can provide. But Westcourt's resources, which consist of two district nurses, two part-time auxilliary nurses and one full-time enrolled nurse, are at present insufficient to provide the twenty-four hour cover which Sheila will need. So Job probably will have to go to a hospice to die, where it will cost more and where, wonderful though the local hospice is, it will not be the same as dying at home.

I say to Maureen when we leave that death is the last great test for us all. She says, 'We have now become experts, particularly in the hospice movement, at controlling pain either through the use of painkillers or "syringe drivers", little devices put just under the skin which release pre-set doses of pain killer into the blood stream. For most people the last stages of death from terrible diseases like cancer are now relatively easy and painless – the pain killers get stronger and stronger, the patient gets drowsier and drowsier until they slip quietly into death. It is in the period before the last phase of life that they need a lot of care. Some become peaceful and contented when they know they are going to die. Some withdraw, turn their faces to the wall and cease human contact. Some become agitated and angry. It is at this moment that the role of the doctor ends and that of the nurse begins. Naturally we don't prescribe the drugs, we merely suggest them. But it's now up to us to provide the care that is necessary. Nurses are not just doctor's assistants; they have a separate and special job in the business of caring and it is at this stage in the process of dying that we come into our own.'

Maureen tells me that at Westcourt, each specialist service in the surgery, including those who provide spiritual healing and alternative medicine in this very unusual practice, see themselves as part of a team with a single aim – making their patients feel better.

I had arrived at Westcourt surgery earlier that morning and sat in with Dr John Latham as he saw his patients. John has come to believe that healing is more than a physical transaction between doctor and patient and that understanding the causes of illness and the process of healing requires a 'holistic' approach, which is what he and most of his fellow doctors at Westcourt seek to provide. He also thinks that this approach makes not only for better medicine and healthier patients, but could save the NHS money as well.

I ask him to explain exactly what he means by 'holistic', which many patients might see as just another term of mystery and mumbo-jumbo, when all they want the doctor to do is to make them better. He replies, 'Healing is a process. It begins with the recognition of the need for it. It continues with the partial surrender of ourselves to another person or directly to God. Because that is what the patient asks for when he or she comes to me, I have to be aware of that need and that surrender. I then must recognise that person's ability to self heal, which some people call homeostasis, as well as their possible need for help. This help may come in one of several ways – by being listened to; by being touched; by the doctor or therapist being himself; by being loved; by being accepted; by being understood; by empathy; by catharsis. There are times, of course, when my job is simply to act as a mechanic and mend the broken part. But there are other times when my job is to be a kind of consultant who helps a person to understand their own health and how to maintain it.'

Sally, one of the patients in the waiting room, tells me that she likes coming here because she feels the doctors really listen. 'Only one of them reaches for the prescription pad as soon as you go in,' she says. John Latham tells me that he knows surgeries where a buzzer sounds outside to call the next patient, who goes in to find the doctor sitting, back to the patient, writing and silent. The patient sits and waits until the doctor, pen hovering over the prescription pad, asks what is wrong. John Latham believes that the process of healing begins when the doctor greets the patient in the waiting room. He always goes to collect his patient personally and first shakes them by the hand. Touch is an important part of the process. John's prescription pad remains out of sight in a drawer.

Dr Craig Brown, one of John Latham's colleagues at West Court, has been doing some research into spiritual healing and alternative medicine at the surgery. He works with Brenda Watters and Del Ralph, two spiritual healers who run a clinic for patients, and the doctors who want to use their services. Craig says that those who receive spiritual healing don't necessarily feel less pain but they do often feel better. I am present when Del sees Ruby. She describes her condition as living through black tunnels of despair. She has been to eight sessions with Del and is now feeling better, though she is not yet convinced that the healing has had any effect – it could be just one of her remissions.

The practice also uses the services of a professional counsellor, Mary Verghese. Mary works for three local practices and is often able to help patients either as a complementary process to the doctor's actions or when the doctor has reached the end of their healing resources and needs extra help. Typically, many patients go to see their doctor with what appears to be a physical problem, but this just hides a deeper emotional one that has to be discovered and dealt with. I see this in practice while sitting in with John Latham. One woman comes in complaining of a pain in her side but it very soon becomes clear that her real problem is a pathological horror of cancer and she just wants her doctor to reassure her. Another, an ex-policeman who served in Brighton, comes in with a severe form of eczema on the feet. Dr John explains to him that this is often a bodily sign of inner stress and out tumbles, unbidden, a personal problem of massive proportions, dating back to the stresses he was subject to when a member of the CID team investigating the Brighton bomb attack on the Conservative Conference in 1984.

We also see a remarkable and voluble Irishman called Leo who has a bit of a drink problem and a wonderful line in home-spun philosophy. 'The problem with our society,' he says, 'is that we value money and use people, when what we need is a society which uses money and values people.' John comments after he has gone that maybe that is the problem with our health system, too.

Craig Brown says that the important thing is to measure the effect of the healing process by what happens, not what the doctor can explain. 'There are all sorts of things that doctors can't explain but which nevertheless appear to work: acupuncture and homeopathy are two examples. Far too many doctors think that, if modern Western medicine isn't practising it and they can't explain it, then it isn't worth doing. If we had a little more humility as doctors we might be a bit better at healing. We often rely far too much on drugs,' Craig says. He thinks that the important thing in healthcare is to measure patient outcomes not drug and medical inputs, and is developing a quality of life indicator which can be used to assess the success of the Westcourt practice on the basis of how the patients feel, rather than how the doctors think they are doing.

This year, Craig Brown ran two clinics for stress. One was for teenagers taking exams. Basically, he explains, they were teaching people meditation techniques – not that he had called them that; it would have put people off. The response had been phenomenal, especially from the school children. His daughter Karen tells me, as we sit having tea in their garden, that the pupils who had gone to the sessions thought they were 'great'. Craig says, 'I can't think of many things better designed to save the Health Service money in the future than teaching young people how to cope with stress at an early age.'

The effects of the 'holistic' approach being followed by Westcourt may be having results in other areas, too. The drug bill for the surgery is a full 9 per cent below the national average. This amounts to a potential saving to the National Health Service, in this surgery alone, of £70,000 annually.

Westcourt has joined the new budget holding system being introduced by the Government. Almost all those I spoke to thought it was a good thing for Westcourt, but that it may not be a good thing for the Health Service as a whole. Over lunch, Jane Birchfield, Westcourt's fundholding manager, and Matthew Taylor Robertson, the partner responsible for fundholding matters, tell me that holding their own budget has given Westcourt staff the freedom to be innovative and try new procedures. Matthew tells me that he doubts whether the Government could afford to allow every practice to follow Westcourt's example.

When Westcourt converted to a fund-holding practice, they received an annual management allowance of £34,000 to help with setting up a management system and a further £12,500 to buy a computer system for their 12,000-patient practice. Matthew says, 'It's a good thing for our patients, but I fear it will create a two-tier system – can the Government really afford to do it for everyone?'

Jane is responsible for, among other things, the practice's relations with local hospitals, including private hospitals with whom they can now place contracts. This flexibility is welcome, but, Jane points out, could be used to enable private hospitals to cut their costs so low that they undercut and threaten their local NHS equivalents. 'In one sense, the system is a good one,' Jane says. 'It makes our relationship with the local hospitals very visible – and that enables everyone to see exactly how much things cost and where everyone is coming from. But it is now within our power, by changing referral patterns, to damage the clinical departments of our local NHS hospitals. We in this practice have decided that we don't wish to do that and instead we will use the system to enable us to have a proper purchaser/provider relationship with the local NHS hospital so we can help it improve its services. But how many practices will do the same – and how many NHS hospitals will close if they don't?'

Jane and Matthew also complain about the constant stream of changing regulations coming from the Department of Health. 'We have a good dialogue with our local health authorities. But someone in London seems to spend their entire time writing new instructions which keep dropping through our letter box, weighing pounds at a time, but always three months late. Many of the instructions we receive from London have the scent of whim and dogma about them. In 1990, there was a contract change to encourage health promotion clinics. We in Westcourt are strongly in favour of health education, so we set up around twenty clinic sessions a week to help our patients with diet, hypertension, stress management, obesity, menopause etc. We took on extra staff; our patients responded enthusiastically. And then, two years later we are instructed to stop everything. We are now trying to keep the most important clinics going, but, pretty soon, we will have to consider closing them down and losing staff.'

Ula, a patient waiting to be seen at the anti-natal clinic, complains of the extra bureaucracy of the new system. She is expecting her first child. She also has a painful wrist complaint, for which the doctor had prescribed a splint. She has opted to have her baby at nearby Chichester hospital, so her doctor recommended that she should go there to be fitted with her new splint. But when she went to Chichester, they said that, since she wasn't their regular patient, she must go to her 'home' hospital in Worthing. All this for a cheap and simple splint!

Linda Mitchell, the practice mid-wife, tells me that she is concerned about the effect of the recession on young mothers who are having to return to work far too early after the birth of their babies. This is borne out as I sit with her while she sees patients. The first is Lorraine who describes her unborn first child as 'a right little fidget'. To my astonishment she pulls the scan picture of her child from her bag and I am able to see the head, spinal cord and limbs very clearly. Lorraine tells me that she was a senior secretary and her husband is a mechanical engineer. She will have to return to work as soon as possible after the child is born in order to cover their mortgage payments. Four of the five young mothers I speak to in the maternity clinic say the same thing. Linda says that there is a strong correlation between learning to talk and communicate and the amount of time parents are able to spend with their children in the early weeks and months of life. We are storing up serious medical and social problems for the future because young mothers are forced to return to work too early and do not get enough time to spend with their children.

Linda also tells me that she is in favour of home births in low-risk cases. They are on average cheaper than hospital births, which cost £250 pounds for every day the mother is in the maternity ward. But there are not enough midwives to provide every eligible patient with a choice of home birth. Indeed, there was not even the equipment to do these safely until one of the local midwives raised several hundred pounds to purchase the vital equipment they needed for home births by walking over the South Downs.

In the evening we go back to John Latham's beautiful house by Rustington beach and swim in the sea before an extended and amusing dinner with his wife Carol and their children, Richard, who is a gardener, and Mike and Mandy who are following their father and mother into medicine and nursing.

On the following day I have to return to London but before I go, I have an opportunity to talk to Sylvia Sere, Westcourt's practice manager. Sylvia, who has had wide experience in the business field, was recently recruited and has been running the practice for just a few months. She says, 'This is, in effect, a small business with a turnover of well over half a million pounds a year – and that doesn't include the drug and prescription budget. Practices often recruit their manager from within the Health Service and they often don't have the previous business experience to enable them to manage this kind of operation effectively. I had quite a challenge persuading staff here that change in certain areas of office organisation would be beneficial at Westcourt, resulting in better value for money. Across the country large sums are at risk of being wasted because of inefficiency, which could better be used for patient care.'

Driving back from Littlehampton to London through Sussex countryside glowing with summer, I reflect on what a long journey it has been from the bleakness of Hartcliffe and Withywood in November – and how much I have learned between the two.

Conclusions

◆

The state of Britain

The descriptions of the visits which are contained in this book are anecdotal. And so, necessarily, are the conclusions.

In many ways the most interesting conversations and insights I had were out of the work place and in informal chats with those who were kind enough to spend time with me. I do not pretend that it is possible to draw all-embracing political conclusions, or to write a universal manifesto, from what I have seen and heard. I retain a kaleidoscope of impressions which are not easily organised into one coherent set of arguments – a bit like life itself. Nevertheless, I am left with some powerful impressions about the state of Britain today.

The first is that Britain is in a profoundly depressed and bewildered state. There is a deep and almost tangible sense of a hope that has died and of a leadership that has failed. The eighties seemed to be a decade when we grasped at national solutions and thought we were beginning to solve some of the country's underlying problems. That is now revealed to have been an illusion. We are back where we were and none of the solutions which promised so much have delivered the answers we were looking for. There is a dangerous mood of fatalism in Britain – a loss of national self-confidence and even self-respect.

The second impression is that people are desperately looking for a lead – and not just from the Government. Most people I spoke to seem to recognise that there are powerful challenges and difficult decisions ahead. But politicians do not seem to be addressing them. Indeed, they seem to be avoiding them. The political parties seek votes on the basis that the problems do not exist at election time and play the Westminster game on the assumption that they do not have to be confronted in Parliament.

Where things have been achieved, as with the miners of Monkton-hall, or the Eldonian co-operators, they have been achieved very often despite the politicians, not because of them. There is a strong feeling that politics – the whole of politics – has failed. I expected to find anger with the Government; and I did. What I did not expect to discover was that there is anger and disillusionment with the opposition parties, too. A woman in East London said to me, 'What on earth are you there for, if you cannot stop this lot doing what they are doing?' One of David Walters' weavers reflected the view of many when he said, 'Why don't you ever get your act together. You are all as bad as each other. I don't want to trust my children's future to you lot. You think only of yourselves.'

The third conclusion is that Westminster is seen as increasingly irrelevant. During almost all my visits, Westminster was obsessed by the long-running internal battle over Maastricht. For most people this was simply incomprehensible and bewilderingly irrel-evant, when they were losing their jobs, struggling with their mortgages and trying desperately to ensure that their businesses survived. In so far as people were interested in Maastricht, they were angry about being denied a say in the process through a referendum. But chiefly, Westminster's laws are seen as at best an obstruction and at worst positively damaging. There is a sense that when we pass laws in Westminster, we do it without knowing the effect it will have on those whose livelihoods will be affected – a view reflected equally on the deck of the *Silver Harvester*, and in the classrooms of the schools in Peckham and Newbury and on the wooded hillsides of the Wye valley. Westminster seems to speak in a language most people do not understand and with which they cannot associate themselves. There is generally a high opinion of MPs for their local work. But no one is at all convinced by the shouting and the over-heated rhetoric in Parliament, except as a kind of running political soap opera which is enter-taining to watch but irrelevant to the real things that matter. In short, the gap between Government and governed in Britain is dangerously wide and getting wider.

And yet, there is often a readiness to do the difficult things that are necessary. I found it in the extraordinary courage of ordinary people driving unprotected relief lorries in Bosnia, who were prepared to risk their lives to do something, because

Western governments were doing so little; in the workers of Toyota and Johnson Control, who were willing to learn practices and processes which their previous bosses would never have dared to ask of them and their trades unions would have protected them against; in the residents of Adur, who seem to understand better than the Government that it is worth paying a little more in order to respond to the threat to our common environment; and in the willingness of young black fathers in North Peckham to start tackling the crime and drugs which are blighting the future for their children.

I am left with the feeling that we, as politicians, consistently underestimate the understanding and sense of common purpose of those whom we seek to lead. People are much more ready to make sacrifices for what they regard to be the common good than we politicians have allowed ourselves to believe. At the end of a strongly materialist 'me-first' decade, I think it is even possible to detect a new mood of counter-materialism in Britain. But there seems to be no one to lead it.

This new mood is especially evident in our sense of community which remains strong and now seems to be growing again, even after nearly half a century in which governments of all colours have sought increasingly to centralise our institutions at the expense of the local dimension. What hope there is in Britain is to be found not in our formal national institutions, but in our informal and voluntary structures and, especially, in our local communities. What has struck me is how often I have found solutions being practically worked out at local level to problems which seem to us in Westminster to be insoluble. For instance, I suspect that no problem more affects the everyday life and freedoms of people in this country than the rise and rise of criminality and the breakdown of law and order. We have tried all sorts of things at Westminster. What we have failed to recognise, as Ollie Goode and the Solihull Crime Reduction Programme have done, is that crime is a complex matter which *must* be tackled on a long-term basis by mobilising the whole community.

Similarly, we in Parliament have argued over what should be done about the declining competitiveness of Britain's coal industry. In Monktonhall they have halved coal production prices through owning their own jobs – but rather than helping them and assisting more miners to follow their example, Parliament has instead opted for more subsidies to enable the old practices of British Coal to continue for a little longer.

In Orkney and in County Tyrone, they have begun to work out how to use the new technologies to overcome the problems of rural education and deprivation, but there is no sign yet of a national programme to enable other rural communities to benefit from their new thinking. In Oxford, the gay and lesbian community have come together to provide the practical help and compassion for people with Aids which, it seems, our society at large still finds it impossible to provide. In Peckham in London and in Hartcliffe and Withywood in Bristol, if not yet in Toxteth and Moss Side, people are beginning to regenerate and renew their own communities from within, having learnt that little will be achieved by relying on experts from outside. The pioneers of 'planning for real' are finding that people not only have the right, but also the ability to participate in the planning decisions which will shape the community in which they live – and that if they do participate, the result can be beneficial for the developer and for the people who will live there, alike.

I have one final impression from these visits. It is of a deeply divided country. There are now parts of Britain, and I have only seen a few of them, which are so sunk in poverty, lawlessness and despair that they are, effectively, not part of our country at all. I had no idea what things are really like in Peckham and Toxteth and Moss Side until I went to stay there. I recall as a boy in Northern Ireland, wandering the back streets of Belfast, seeing the poverty, the discrimination and the hopelessness and knowing with absolute certainty that my country, Northern Ireland, faced a terrible nemesis yet to come. Over these last few months, I have seen the same – and even worse – conditions in our inner cities. I now find myself obsessed by the thought that what I saw as a boy in Belfast was not something unique to that city and its religious conflicts, but merely the signs of a society in a more advanced state of decay than that of mainland Britain. Whatever we do, we will ultimately fail to provide any kind of better future for our country unless we can find the means to rescue those of our fellow citizens who live in such poverty, dereliction and fear and give them the chance to hope again. I do not believe that this will be successfully achieved by us doing things for them, but by giving them the means to do things for themselves – as Winston Simpson pointed out to me in Moss Side. But I have no doubt that unless we succeed in this, then we will fail in everything else.

What could be done

Politics and Government

In considering how to improve the condition of our country it is necessary first to recognise that Westminster is not one of the solutions, it has become one of the problems. Westminster is out of date, out of ideas and out of touch. It is structured for confrontation in an age when success will increasingly lie in partnership. It conducts its affairs in what most people see as incomprehensible mumbo-jumbo ritual. And it speaks in a language which only those who live inside the charmed circle of Westminster understand. Perhaps all this was perfectly appropriate in an age when we had trust in a paternalistic Establishment, when we could be assured of rising prosperity and when our position in the world enabled us to shape events, rather than having them shaped for us. But these days have gone. We are now facing immense and very difficult challenges in our country and most people I met on these visits understand this, even if too many politicians don't: how do we hold our society together against the background of relative decline measured by the new rising economies of the Far East? How do we maintain competitiveness in a total global economy in which we have to compete head to head with nations which have much lower social and labour costs? How do we adapt our social spending in order to maintain a cohesive society, while earning our living abroad? How do we alter our lifestyles so as to respond to the urgent global threat to our environment? How do we preserve our national sovereignty and even identity, whilst committing ourselves to the international institutions necessary to maintain peace in an increasingly unstable and interdependent world?

Westminster and Whitehall, in their present forms, are simply incapable of providing sensible answers to these questions. Our institutions of Government will have to be modernised and opened up. Government will have to concentrate less on telling people what to do and more on enabling them to do things for themselves. It will have to understand that decisions made by closed circles of experts are frequently bad decisions, not good ones and that to involve those affected by decisions more, as they do in 'planning for real', can result in better decisions, not worse ones. Above all, Westminster and Whitehall will have to recognise that success comes from creating the structures necessary for co-operation not from preserving institutionalised confrontation, as the management and workforce in Toyota in Derby have shown.

I have long wondered whether political institutions shape the institutions of commerce and the work place, or whether the truth is not the other way round; whether it wasn't the impact of the industrial revolution which forced the franchise reforms of the nineteenth century; the emergence of mass production and collective power which gave birth to mass politics in this century. If I am right, then it cannot be without significance that the new firms which are succeeding, such as Toyota and Johnson Control, are doing so by dismantling the strong vertical hier-archies and command structures of the old industries and replac-ing them with a style of management which is participatory, encourages thinking, values its workforce, operates on consensus and encourages lateral networking. If that is the future, then our style of politics seems peculiarly out of tune with our age.

Lastly, Westminster and Whitehall are going to have to surren-der some of their power. This country will not solve its problems unless we can unleash the power and imagination of Britain's communities. It is here that the new energies and new thinking lie; that the new ideas and the practical solutions are being worked out. It is here that people have shown, as in Solihull and Liverpool and Monktonhall, that they want to make their contribution.

We have created a society which has a culture of dependency, not just in its welfare system but in its politics, too. This is not the fault of the citizens of Britain; it is the fault of our politicians. It has suited us politicians to pretend that we could solve every problem and give everyone more. But those days, if they ever existed, are now over. Britain's future will be as much decided outside our borders as inside them: in Brussels; in the world money markets; in questions of peace and war over which we nowadays have relatively little influence; in the pollution from a nuclear power station a thousand miles away whose existence we do not even know about.

But the expectations which it still suits national politicians to encourage have remained the same. And so, politicians can hardly complain when something goes wrong, that it is – to invert the phrase of Eammon Kearney of JCA – not 'your fault', or 'my fault', or even 'our fault', but *'their* fault' – *'them'* being the Government.

The paradox is that by preserving the atmosphere of self importance and the illusion of absolute power, Parliament has only succeeded in making itself weaker and weaker. A strong Parliament – and we desperately need a strong Parliament – would start by recognising its own limitations. Meanwhile, the old 'contract' between politician and voter is, itself, beginning to break down and we are going to have to build a new one to replace it. The difficult actions we are going to have to take in the future will only be possible in a democratic society if we are able to let people understand the facts and give them the means to be part of the decisions, wherever this is possible. This means recognising that, for most people in this country, there is as much sense of identity with their community as there is with the central state and that this should be encouraged, not suppressed. It means allowing different communities to find their own different solutions to problems which ought to be more their province to solve, than that of Westminster. It means encouraging pluralism and promoting success wherever it appears instead of imposing uniformity and dogmas from the top. It means, as with the Eldonians and the inhabitants of the Waterfield Estate in Hounslow, giving people a sense of ownership of change, rather than importing experts to impose change on them.

The most difficult problem to solve in building a new contract between politician and voter is that of taxation. People seem less and less inclined to give politicians a blank cheque with their money. This scepticism on tax has expressed itself in recent elections in Britain and elsewhere as a competition about which party can offer the lowest taxation. I do not believe that future success for Britain lies in excessively high levels of tax that remove incentives and trap individuals at marginal tax rates. But if politics in the future is merely to be a competition as to who can offer the lowest taxation, then none of the things I want to see happen in Britain can be achieved and very few of the problems which I have described in this book can be tackled. But I wonder whether we have accurately read the message which the electorate is sending us on tax? People may like low taxes, but every indicator shows that they value our public system of education, health and welfare services as well.

I suspect that the real question about taxation is not just about how low it is, but what value people feel they get from the taxes they pay and what control they have to ensure that their taxation wishes are carried out. They fear (with some justification) that, once their money falls into the Government's hands, it will be spent not on the things that individual taxpayers value, but on those which satisfy the Government's political ideologies. And they believe (again with justification) that a lot of their money will be wasted in government bureaucracy and inefficiency.

If we are to win the argument for the investments which Britain needs to solve its problems, then we politicians are going to have to find a new language of taxation which relates cost to opportunity, which concentrates on value for taxation as much as on tax levels and which places some constraints on the freedom which governments enjoy in the way that the people's taxes are spent. Earmarking, or hypothecating, taxation is one way to do this (e.g. the Liberal Democrats' 1 penny for education at the last election).

Part of the task of convincing people that they are getting value for taxation is to provide value for government. Government is, at its heart, a service industry. But it doesn't behave like that. So far the huge strides towards quality customer service made by most of the modern service industries seem to have passed the process of government by, except in a few pioneering local councils. The Citizen's Charter project, launched by the Prime Minister, is a start in the right direction but rather a small one. We need to change the whole culture of government so that it measures its effectiveness not by the work that is put in, but by the results that are achieved; so that success is measured in terms of improvements in quality of life. Westcourt surgery is a tiny example of the revolution in attitude which started in the private sector, but which is now spreading to some corners of the public service, too. It is time that Government caught up.

And finally, Government must learn that its role in the future will be to dictate less and enable more. One of the clearest messages to come out of these visits for me is about the importance of partnership. The theory that governments can do everything has, thank goodness, been abandoned everywhere except the darkest corners of the extreme left. But there are still many who believe that the role of government is to do nothing, or at least as little as possible. This is equally damaging, as we have seen over the last decade. Government, at all levels, is a very large player in the fabric of modern nations. It employs a substantial proportion of the workforce and deploys huge sums of money. It cannot stand aside. But where it does intervene, it should do so as far as possible on the basis that it is doing things with individuals and communities, not for them.

Economics

We have to start modernising Britain's economy and industrial structure.

Haley Dosser, David Walters' sales director, is right. We have two ways to go. Either we can compete, as a low-wage, low-value-added, low-skill economy, with the other low-wage low-skill economies – in which case Britain's future is going to be a particularly uncomfortable one. Or we can do what David Walters have done; capitalise on our skills and go up market into high-value-added goods and high-skill production. To succeed where Walters and Toyota and Johnson Controls have succeeded means a new style of management. It means valuing your workforce, it means education and training and learning new skills. And it means understanding that we live and must trade in an increasingly open and global world economy. There is no refuge for Britain in saying, as some of those who sought Toyota's supply contracts said, 'we are improving'. Until our products are up to world standards, we will not trade successfully in world markets. I suspect that, of all the changes Britain has to make, those necessary to survive in the emerging global economy are the most necessary and will be the most difficult.

Internally too, our economy will have to be much more efficient in utilising natural resources. We can never generate our full industrial and economic potential whilst the economic contribution of so many of our citizens is lost through permanent unemployment. The work being pioneered by the Industrial Society in bringing people like Charles back into the workforce in Safeways at Wapping is vital, not just from a human point of view, but also because it means that economic talent from which the national economy can benefit is no longer wasted. But the real dividend in providing new jobs will come from creating a much more flexible economy; one in which people will be encouraged to work in every nook and cranny of the economic structure and in whatever way their individual personal circumstances allow at the time. Oliver Johnson of the Industrial Society is right – work will be a 9 to 5, eighteen to sixty affair for fewer and fewer people in the future. We will have to change our welfare system so that it encourages flexible and part-time working, rather than penalising it in the way experienced by Dawn in Hartcliffe and Withywood. We will have to find a way to establish a basic minimum framework of employment protection for part-time workers which does not inhibit the creation of jobs in the part-time sector. Retirement must also increasingly be seen not as an event, but as a process. What we need is a flexible decade of retirement which allows people who are reaching the end of their careers to retire at a pace which suits them, rather than being placed on the economic scrap heap on their sixtieth or sixty-fifth birthday. We must open up much greater opportunities for self employment and small enterprise, not just for the middle class, but especially for people like the trainee black painters and decorators whom I met in Camden. We will need to change our economic culture in order to encourage risk taking. And Government should be encouraging a public/private partnership to invest in the creation of a national network of information 'highways' which will enable everyone to use the new technologies in the ways they are experimenting with on

Hoy and in Omagh; so that people can make their economic contribution, wherever they live, or whatever stage of their life cycle they are at. This is something of especial importance to women, whose economic potential is being terribly wasted at present.

Efficiency in human terms needs to be matched by efficiency in our use of raw materials, especially of energy. Our present profligacy in consuming and wasting finite resources is imposing a double penalty on our economy – the first through inefficiency and the second through pollution. Our past governments have claimed that being environmentally conscious is something our economy cannot afford. The opposite is true. The efficient advanced economies of the future will be clean economies, recycling precious raw materials, encouraging efficient energy usage and limiting pollution and environmental degradation. Japan, for instance, has very high energy costs, but is probably the world's most successful and competitive economy, while in the failed economies of the Soviet Union and Eastern Europe, energy prices were kept low, encouraging high-energy-use industries to flourish artificially and cause massive pollution problems.

Fortunately, the British public seems to understand better than most of our politicians the need to conserve and protect our environment. If we are serious about recycling 25 per cent of our waste by the year 2000, then the kind of scheme which I saw in Adur ought not to be an interesting exception, but encouraged to become the common practice everywhere. But, as Martin King in Adur said, recycling will not be enough. We are going to have to reduce profligate consumption. This will mean using market and price systems to encourage greater efficiency, for instance in energy, where the price of fossil fuels will have to rise in order to conserve stocks and provide greater incentives for energy saving and efficiency.

One of the effects of encouraging energy efficiency through the price and market systems will be to give a boost to developing Britain's renewable energy potential. These islands are calculated to have Europe's greatest potential for renewable energy exploitation through wind and wave power – but this is being largely wasted at present.

But encouraging this will not be easy, and the task has not

been made any easier by the Government's action in imposing a crude and indiscriminate tax on the most vulnerable consumer in the form of VAT on domestic fuel, with no help to households to become more energy efficient and no purpose other than revenue raising. There is a difference between taxing the vulnerable to bail out the Government and encouraging energy efficiency to save the environment.

And finally, if we are to carry the tough environmental legislation that is necessary to create greater efficiency and less environmental damage, we politicians are going to have to carry people with us. There is no point in drawing up rules in the name of conservation which are either unworkable or counter productive where they have to be applied, as I found out on the deck of the *Silver Harvester* and in the hills above the Wye Valley.

Education

Education is the key to building an economy which will succeed or fail, depending on its capacity to unlock individual potential. Unless Britain can find the means and the will to invest in creating an education system which will ensure that children like Michael Dadze are not overlooked and every one of the children in Sadie's class in the Peckham school gets the same chances as those at Shaw House, Newbury, then we can never succeed.

Our present education system is dreadfully failing those who need it most. Half a million children a week in Britain now play truant because education does not seem to offer them anything. And our education system is failing our economy, too. It is far too specialised, as every single one of the industrialists to whom I spoke made clear. We need to build a much more flexible education system, based on a good grounding in the basics and a much more rounded education in later years.

This means starting early by giving every three and four-year-old an opportunity to receive high-quality pre-school education. One way of doing this would be through a voucher system for early years education which parents could cash in at a local play group, nursery school or any other approved institution of their choice. Money invested in these very early years is repaid many times over later in the education process. Studies in the US have shown that every $1 invested in a year's pre-school education returns a benefit of $7 during the education process and in later life – one of the most significant savings being in the prevention of crime.

We must also help parents to become partners with their children's teachers in their children's education, so that what happens in the home re-enforces what is being taught in the school: I believe most parents are much more interested in knowing how to help their own children learn than they are in participating in the administration of their school.

We must be prepared to put increased resources and more teachers into those areas, like Peckham, where the need is greater and where education provides the only escape route from the trap of poverty and deprivation.

But spending more on education, as I believe we must, will have to be accompanied by getting greater value for the money we spend. Teachers and the educational establishment must realise that measuring outcomes applies to them, too. The Government is, in principle, right in seeking to find a way to measure teaching success, especially in the basics, even if the means they have chosen to do this are wrong in practice. I see nothing wrong with tests and the publication of results, provided these are done in a fair, sensible and accurate way that is designed to help pupils, teachers and parents.

Broadening our curriculum and establishing a more flexible exam system, especially at A and degree levels, is a vital step towards establishing a more broad-based education system. We need to complete the process of breaking down the barriers between vocational and academic qualifications. A-levels and degrees should be credit based, so that people have the chance to develop their own potential and build on their success in a flexible way which suits their opportunities and abilities.

Above all, we must build a 'second chance' education system, with a strong adult education and re-training sector. The use of the new technologies, like Kirkwall Grammar's 'white board' system, used in conjunction with the Open University, could offer every adult in the land the chance to re-train or re-educate themselves at a time of their choice at least once in their adult lives.

Meanwhile our training system is a mess and must be reformed. There are at present in Britain 160 professional standard-setting bodies and sixty separate examination and validation organisations, backed up by innumerable vocational qualifications. And our benefits system, as I saw in the Camden training centre, actually discourages some from re-training and bettering themselves. This is a nonsense at a time when there are so many people on the dole and so much talent is going to waste.

And instead of having our training administered by a muddle of quangos and a confusion of Government bodies, we should bring it under one umbrella, perhaps through a network of local chambers of trade which have 'public law status' as they do in France and Germany to which all local businesses in an area would be required to pay a levy. In this way, local businesses could ensure that they are training for skills which are needed and they would have a powerful and unified voice which would command the attention of local and national governments.

Law and order

Reported crime now stands at record levels. While the Government has introduced over sixty-four separate pieces of law and order legislation since 1979, the number of crimes recorded each year by the police has risen by over 120 per cent. Young people represent a horrifying proportion of these crime totals. A quarter of all known offenders are under seventeen, and a further quarter are between seventeen and twenty-one. The average age of a housebreaker is sixteen-and-a-half, and one young man in four has a caution or a conviction by his twenty-first birthday.

But, as the Home Office's own figures show, the level of recorded crime and the number of known offenders are only the tip of the iceberg. Of the fifteen million household burglaries committed in 1992, for example, only seven million were recorded by the police. For every hundred crimes, fifty are reported, thirty are recorded, seven are cleared up, and only two result in convictions. Yet the amount of money we spend directly on preventing crime is tiny. Out of the total Criminal Justice Budget in 1992–93 of £8.7 billion, the Home Office spends just £15.6 million (0.18 per cent) on crime prevention.

Of course, tackling this huge problem means ensuring that there is an efficient and appropriate system of punishment in place for the criminals who now terrorise the lives of so many of our citizens. But, as Ollie Goode in Solihull, Brad in Peckham and Paul Hurst in Toxteth realise, solving Britain's crime problem is more complex than that.

If we want to begin to tackle the kind of lawlessness there is in Moss Side, the police will have to be prepared to do more of what Brad and Paul are doing in Toxteth and Peckham; getting involved with the community, not just sending raiding parties into it from outside. And politicians are going to have to stop judging the police just by the raw figures of arrests. Arrest and crime clear-up rates are an important measure of police success. But the work Brad and Paul are doing is quite as difficult and in the end just as valuable.

We cannot seriously hope to tackle problems such as those in Peckham unless we are prepared to give the police adequate resources and manpower. The cost involved in this could be considerable. But I am quite convinced that this is one price people are prepared to pay, rather than having to resort to vigilantes as many communities at the front edge of the crime wave are increasingly having to do. And we in Parliament, when we draft legislation, must think how it will affect the practice of policing on the ground. There are few clearer examples of Westminster's recent failures than that we gaily passed a series of measures over the last fourteen years which we are now having to repeal because they have made life both more difficult and more dangerous for policemen in our inner cities.

But in the end, sheer police numbers will not solve crime. The battle has to be a continuous and long-term one. It must start in school, and in the family, where the crucial first lines of defence are built. And it must continue in our homes, work places and communities right throughout our working lives. We should be putting much more emphasis on crime prevention, from designing opportunities for crime out of our buildings and public spaces, to putting photos on cheque and credit cards, to providing locks and window catches for those who are most vulnerable. The fight against crime has to involve everyone. Mobilising support against crime across the whole community, as they are doing in Solihull, ought to be the task of the authorities in every community in Britain.

Finally, the battle against crime requires a clear and focused strategy and an accurate means of measuring success. We should focus first on the high-crime areas, like Moss Side, where normal life has almost disappeared, and on the high-risk groups like women, who are most likely to be victims. And we should be able to measure the success of what we do in precise terms, so that we know which actions return the best results.

Inner cities

The task of regenerating Britain's inner cities is one of the most urgent and most difficult that confronts us. But it will not be achieved simply by money. It is essential that inner city communities feel that they have ownership of and a stake in the renewal of their own communities. We should be encouraging the growth of co-operatives like the Eldonians whenever the task is that of knocking down old houses and building new ones. It should be a cardinal rule of every inner city redevelopment that contractors should have to train and employ local youngsters from the community that is being improved. And no plan for redevelopment should be allowed to be implemented unless, using techniques like 'planning for real', local people have had a say in its formulation. It is through a sense of control over their own space, and a pride in their own housing, that many people become confident enough to take the first steps out of isolation into the community.

But if we are to encourage community-based development of the sort which has happened in Eldonian Liverpool and is beginning to happen in Brick Lane, East London, then we are going to have to create the economic institutions to support them. At present, results come haphazardly and are often hindered by politicians, rather than helped by them. The Government's programmes are good as far as they go. But there is too much policy by initiative, too little long-term strategic direction and too many useful projects started in inner cities over the last few years using Government money, which will collapse as short-term funding is withdrawn. We should be establishing in Britain a network of community-funded institutions, including community banks, through whom funding can be channelled for community-based initiatives. Another vital ingredient in stimulating local initiative is to give communities access to cheap, independent legal, technical and commercial expertise.

And we will have to create the political institutions to provide accountability and support for these initiatives. Britain's inner-city regeneration programmes are run without any kind of accountability to the communities they are supposed to be helping. If we are to re-create a sense of civic pride in Britain, we can only do it through civic institutions which are accountable and strong enough to create the partnerships with central government and private industry which are essential for successful programmes of regeneration. This means reversing the centralisation of power which has been going on in this country for nearly half a century and strengthening the structures of local government and local democracy.

But we will never succeed in regenerating our inner cities until we have made them once again a place in which to live, rather than just a place in which to work. Whilst encouraging private enterprise is always going to be essential so as to provide the wealth upon which our cities and their people depend, we cannot abandon our cities wholly to the private sector and hope for the best. There has also to be an effective instrument for strategic planning and for the provision of public goods as well as private profit. I am especially concerned at the growth and power of the giant commercial retailers. There is, at present, a bias on the part of the government in favour of the developers. The result is all too often the destruction of the local environment, the death of small retail shops and erosion of local services which give human scale, local convenience and greater choice to many of our communities. The balance needs to be redressed, so that we place the same weight on enhancing our common wealth as we do on encouraging private profit.

At the heart of this lies the question of transport. The paradox in Britain today is that most people would do anything but give up their cars. And yet the car in Britain's inner cities does more to damage the quality of life and to ghettoise city communities than anything else. Roads in London are now so crowded that the average speed of traffic in the centre of the city is actually slower today than it was in the days of the horse and carriage at the turn of the century. We are going to have to grasp the nettle by limiting the use of cars in our inner cities and starting to build effective public transport systems.

Rights and responsibilities

The rights of the citizens of our country have to be strengthened to prevent discrimination and the haphazard application of our laws. But with rights go responsibilities – a fact which has been ignored by the Left for far too long. We need a Bill of Rights in Britain which safeguards the basic rights of every citizen, whatever their gender or sexuality, colour or creed or age. And we need a written constitution, protected by a supreme court, which limits the power of both Parliament and the Executive.

But, as Kevin Clare of the Oxford gay and lesbian community pointed out, the greatest safeguard against prejudice and discrimination lies in education. It cannot be in the interests of our children that they should grow up in the age of Aids without an understanding of the nature of our different sexualities, or that they should be ignorant of the different cultures which exist in our multi-ethnic society, or oblivious to the duties as well as the enjoyments of citizenship.

Nor can it be in the interests of our society that we should ignore the importance of the family, particularly as the 'traditional' family is giving way to one-parent and more flexible family structures. If a stable family background and parental nurturing are important to the development of our future citizens, then we have to be prepared to recognise that by giving support to the family, in whatever form it takes, in our social structures and welfare systems. I dread to think what problems and expense we are storing up for ourselves in the future by bringing up children without effective support in the footloose single-parent structures which exist in Moss Side and elsewhere; and by the pressures on people like Lorraine in the Westcourt surgery to return to work early at the cost of contact with her newly born child.

I do not believe that all people are equal, except in three

respects: we are all equal before God; we must all be equal before the law and we should all have equal opportunities. It is the job of Government to ensure the last two of these. This means acting positively to prevent discrimination, to open up access and to spread opportunity. And spreading opportunity means being prepared to target resources, especially educational and child-care resources, towards those who would not otherwise have the same chances as their fellow citizens.

Health

Providing health care at a level which matches people's rising expectations is going to present a major challenge to all the advanced Western democracies in the future. We cannot sustain a position where people look on their doctor as purely a mechanic to put things right when they go wrong. We need to encourage the development of a new partnership between doctors, nurses, carers and their patients in which the health professional acts more and more as a health consultant and patients take some of the responsibility for their own health on their own shoulders.

And doctors are going to have to learn that healing, as John Latham rightly says, is a more complex matter than the administration of drugs. A more holistic approach to health, of the sort that they are beginning to develop at Westcourt, in which doctors see themselves in partnership with others in the healing process, could provide more sickness prevention for the healthy, a higher quality of life for the sick and greater cost efficiency for the Health Service.

We should be looking closely at the opportunities which are now open to us to offer the choice of providing health care in the home where this is appropriate (e.g. in the case of home births and terminal care). In some circumstances this can provide care which is both more personal and less expensive, even when the extra payment to carers and nursing support is taken into account.

No one can ignore the need for greater cost efficiency in our Health Service. But I suspect that there are much greater savings to be made through health education, teaching people the techniques of 'self health', the provision of care in the home, the use of complementary approaches to medicine, tackling bad housing, improving social conditions and, above all, putting a greater emphasis on prevention, than there are through cost cutting and the inappropriate use of management techniques borrowed from the retail sector.

I am broadly in favour of the purchaser/provider split, providing it is sensibly applied. And I favour giving doctors and hospitals more control over their own budgets, especially if this leads to greater accountability, less bureaucracy, and more scope for initiative and experimentation. Unhappily, the Government's NHS reforms seem to be creating just the opposite; more bureaucracy and less accountability. Safeguards will also be needed to ensure that the basic principles and structure of our Health Service are not eroded, as the doctors at Westcourt believe might be happening. And we have to ensure that the business side of these 'health businesses' are properly and efficiently run, with the help of experts in business practices, rather than health professionals diverted to look after a balance sheet.

In the end however, we cannot duck the question of how we resource our National Health Service in the future. With increasing demand and the spiralling costs of medical technology, the NHS is potentially a bottomless pit. People in Britain are angry about cuts in the service, but they consistently vote against the means of delivering greater resources to fund those services – higher taxes.

There is clearly a potential role for earmarked or 'hypothecated' taxes for the health service, which would make clearer the link between the tax paid and the health services received in return.

But we cannot ignore the reality of rationing – or, as some prefer, the 'prioritisation' of health care. The combination of sharply rising numbers of elderly, the increased availability of sophisticated but very expensive treatment options and mounting pressure on scarce public funds make this a problem which cannot be avoided. Previously, rationing has been done, ad hoc, by doctors and waiting lists. Now, the government's health 'reforms' have installed managers and accountants to do the job, even if they pretend otherwise. But, in the state of Oregon in the United States they are experimenting with mechanisms which involve patients and the public in the 'rationing' process. There, a public commission took evidence from health professionals, patients and public and the state legislature then identified 587 out of 709 possible medical treatments which they would fund publicly. The rest were deemed to be medical treatments which should be paid for privately. Amongst the 587 were, for instance, insulin for diabetics, radiotherapy for malignant tumours and appendectomies. Excluded were new-fangled remedies for colds, the removal of benign lumps, etc., which had to be paid for privately. The Oregon experiment has been criticised as crude and flawed, and there are problems with it. On the other hand, we have to recognise that there is already an ad hoc form of rationing in the NHS in Britain, and that we need a more mature debate about how we prioritise demand for health care, and need to involve people in that debate. I would much rather we approached the tough decisions necessary to tackle the rationing problem in an open way, involving the public, than to pretend it is not being done, while setting up systems for the health professionals and bureaucrats to do it behind closed doors.

Britain and the world

The security of our country and the peace which we are able to enjoy cannot be assured from within our shores. The front line of Europe's peace now lies in Bosnia – a fact that is well understood both by our soldiers in the UN force there and by those risking their lives to deliver aid to the front lines. Not one soldier or aid worker I spoke to in Bosnia had any doubt of the necessity and importance of the job they are doing there.

What our soldiers are daily working out in Bosnia are the routines for a new kind of soldiering whose job is to uphold international law, not just to protect Britain's immediate interests. This is not the result of altruism. It is the product of a new realisation that our peace can no longer be defended at our own shore line and can now only adequately be preserved within a framework of international law which we are prepared to defend, even at the risk of our own soldiers' lives.

The record of action, both of the UN and of the European

Community in Bosnia, has been a lamentable one. I greatly fear that the beasts of fascism and destructive nationalism that we thought we had got rid of in Europe almost fifty years ago are loose again. We must learn the lessons of Bosnia and do so quickly. If Western Europe is not prepared to project its power around its borders to preserve peace then this will be a turbulent and dangerous decade for all of us. And, if the international community cannot create the institutions and the will to act to defend the basic tenets of international law and human rights, then there is no chance of preserving peace in a world where the weapons of mass destruction will be more and more widely held and the capacity of individual, even small, nations to wreak havoc through the flow of refugees or through damage to the global environment will be very great.

In the building of the European and world institutions and the establishment of the military professionalism which is necessary to defend these in times of conflict, Britain and her forces have a unique contribution to make. Our soldiers are already making theirs. I fear our leaders have yet some way to go to understand what needs to be done.

Beyond Westminster

I conclude these travels profoundly conscious that we have big problems in this country; but absolutely confident that we have even bigger potential.

Where Britain has succeeded, it wasn't because of governments. Governments did not invent the Spinning Jenny, or build our manufacturing base, or construct the first computer, or discover DNA, or win the World Cup – people did. The Government's job is to bring out initiative, talent and determination – to enable people to develop to the limits of their abilities. Britain's long-term hope lies in creating conditions in which people are free to grow, actively nurtured by our Government; neither constricted by it, nor left to the mercy of the elements.

I started these visits believing what I would find was problems. I have been inspired, instead, by the discovery of so much hope; so many solutions. Two key ingredients of success stand out. The first is the importance of partnership: between police and community; doctor and patient; manager and employee; developer and citizen. And the second is that success seems to come where people and communities take responsibility. Link these two together and I do not believe there is a problem which our country faces which cannot be solved.

That is why I end these journeys an optimist – confident that modernising our country and solving its problems is not beyond the talents of Britain's people; provided only that finding the means to unlock those talents is not beyond the capacity of Westminster.

———————

Index